To Know the Place

Papers presented at Long Island Studies Conference
May 2–3, 1986
Sponsored by Hofstra Cultural Center
and the
Long Island Studies Institute
Hofstra University, Hempstead, Long Island, New York, 11550

Revised and expanded edition.

The Long Island Studies Institute gratefully acknowledges the assistance of the Friends for Long Island's Heritage in the publication of this book.

The Friends for Long Island's Heritage
The Friends for Long Island's Heritage is the citizen support group for Nassau and Suffolk Counties' museum systems. For more than thirty years, the Friends have helped to preserve historic structures, acquire significant museum collections, strengthen museum services, and sponsor special events that interpret Long Island's historical, cultural, and natural heritage. Membership in the Friends for Long Island's Heritage is open to all who are interested in the future of Long Island's educational and cultural resources. For further information, contact the Friends at 1864 Muttontown Road, Syosset, NY 11791; 516–571–7600.

To Know the Place is available at the Hofstra University Bookstore, the gift shops at Old Bethpage Village Restoration (Round Swamp Road, Old Bethpage 11804; 516–572–8415) and the St. James General Store (516-862-8333); at the Weathervane Shop of the Suffolk County Historical Society in Riverhead (300 W. Main Street, Riverhead 11901; 516–727–2881); and from the publisher, Heart of the Lakes, P.O. Box 299, Interlaken, NY 14847 (607–532–4997 or 800–782–9687; fax 607–532–4684).

To Know the Place

Exploring Long Island History

**Edited by Joann P. Krieg and
Natalie A. Naylor**

Revised and expanded edition

Prepared under the auspices of
Hofstra University

Heart of the Lakes Publishing
Interlaken, New York
1995

Library of Congress Cataloguing in Publication Data:
To know the place : exploring Long Island history / edited by Joann
P. Krieg and Natalie A. Naylor : prepared under the auspices of
Hofstra University. — Rev. ed.
  160 p.   cm.
Includes bibliographical reference.
ISBN: 1-55787-128-0
1. Long Island (N.Y.)—History, Local—Study and teaching
  2. Local history—Study and teaching—New York (State)—Long
Island.   I. Krieg, Joann P.   II. Naylor, Natalie A.
F127.L8T57   1995   94–27055
974.7'21'00712—dc20   CIP

Manufactured in the United States of America
Library of Congress Catalogue Number 94–27055
ISBN: 1–55787–128–0

A *quality* publication by
Heart of the Lakes Publishing
Interlaken, NY

Contents

Illustrations

Credits

Anne R. Knight, cover design; David Bunn Martine, drawings on pp. 12, 28; Collections of the Huntington Historical Society, p. 40; John W. Barber and Henry Howe, *Historical Collections of the State of New York* (1841), p. 50, from a copy in the Long Island Studies Institute, Hofstra University; Amityville Historical Society, pp. 67, 71, 72; Parrish Art Museum, 96–99.

Preface

Natalie A. Naylor

These essays originated in the Long Island Studies Conference held at Hofstra University and were originally published by the Long Island Studies Institute in 1986 in a 26–page, 8–1/2"x11" format—the Institute's first publication. Selected other papers from that same conference appeared in *Evoking a Sense of Place*, edited by Joann P. Krieg and published in 1988 by Heart of the Lakes. All of the papers from that conference are available at the Long Island Studies Institute whose collections are now located in the Library Services Center on Hofstra University's West Campus. The Long Island Studies Institute has now published more than a dozen books; this is our first revised edition.

My conference co-director and editor, Joann P. Krieg, Associate Professor of English at Hofstra, first suggested that these particular papers which we thought would be most useful to teachers should constitute a separate publication. We have included not only the papers themselves, but also some supplementary materials. When I realized that the supply of *To Know the Place* was dwindling, we asked the authors to review their original contributions and update for this revised edition.

John Strong virtually rewrote his essay, which had been originally entitled, "From Hunter to Servant: Patterns of Accommodation to Colonial Authority in Eastern Long Island Indian Communities." Laura MacDermeid had described the education program at the Huntington Historical Society where she was then the Museum Curator. She has relocated, but reviewed and revised her article. Rosemary Sloggatt, Director of Education at the Huntington Historical Society, provided an Epilogue, describing changes and current programs. We have again included materials from the pre-visit packet for "A Child's Work and Play" program which have been reset to fit our new format. Charles Howlett added to his essay to indicate the status of the *The Journal of Historical Inquiry* and described the elementary text which developed from the local historical research by high school school students. The original edition of

this book included two examples of student work from their
Journal: "Experiences of World War II Veterans Living in
Amityville"by Noelle Valente (5 [1985]: 28–31) and "The
Amityville Horror: The Facts and Effects" by Patty Muir and
Jennifer Nicholson (6 [1986]: 57–61). We have included here two
different and later examples of work by Amityville high school
students. One essay is on the history of Bethel A. M. E. Church,
one of the oldest African-American congregations on Long
Island, and the other on Amityville as a vacationland, a heritage
it shared with many South Shore communities. I have expanded
and updated the Resources section to include additional
bibliographies. Thus, nearly half of this edition is new material.

As most of us know, Indians are a favorite topic in local
history. It is not always easy, however, for teachers to have access
to recent research in this field, whether by anthropologists or
historians. John Strong's contribution, part of a session devoted
to "Long Island's Native Americans," is an example of the current
research presented at the conference and of continued research
in intervening years. The fact that some Indians were enslaved
and that others were indentured servants is not generally known.
His essay on Indian labor in the post-contact period, focuses on
males who were most likely to appear in the governmental
records.

Thomas J. Schlereth, the keynote speaker at the conference,
cited John Dewey's concept of learning by doing and his belief
that a great deal of education occurs outside the schoolroom. The
essays by Laura MacDermeid and Charles F. Howlett, part of a
conference session entitled "Learning Outside the Classroom,"
exemplify well Dewey's idea of learning by doing, in this case,
"doing" history. Dorothy B. Ruettgers who moderated that
session has written the Introduction. She draws on her many
years of experience teaching social studies in the intermediate
grades to provide some additional suggestions for teachers. Our
title for this book is derived from Professor Schlereth's quotation
of lines from T. S. Eliot's "Little Gidding," in his conference
presentation:

*We shall not cease from exploration
And the end of all our exploring
Will be to arrive where we started
And know the place for the first time.*

This volume should assist teachers and students of all ages
exploring Long Island history and thus to "know the place."

Introduction

Dorothy B. Ruettgers

One of the most challenging tasks in teaching is to make history "come alive" to students who are mostly interested in the here and now and do not wish to concern themselves with the past. An additional problem is that the vast majority of young children have no real sense of time. Fifty years ago and two hundred years are much the same to those who have not lived long enough to remember any changes. The teacher whose curriculum involves local history has the added burden of trying to gather information—an especially difficult task for one who is new to the area. While some communities have a wealth of documented materials, these are not always available or located easily. In many places there is little or no material, or, if there is, it is virtually impossible to distinguish between history and folklore.

Generalizations are the mainstay of many courses or programs which attempt to deal with local history. While some of these all-encompassing ideas may be true, this is often not the case. For example, not all areas on Long Island had Indian settlements, nor did all of its communities have participants in the Revolutionary or Civil Wars (some communities did not even come into existence until the twentieth century). Generalities, whether major or minor, can be false for any given area.

In many classrooms where local history is being introduced, the study of Native Americans becomes of paramount importance. The tendency often is to assume that all East Coast Indians were alike, but Professor John Strong's article provides pertinent information about Long Island Indians. Strong makes use of primary and secondary sources to deal with the interaction between the region's Indians and the settlers. Since his emphasis is on the work of Indians for Europeans, he presents an aspect differing from the more usual accumulation of facts on food, clothing, and customs, which all too often is the only information given to the student. Strong's essay can be useful to teachers who then can select from it the facts most appropriate to their classes. The extensive bibliography on "Long Island's Native American

Indians" in Natalie Naylor's Resources section in this book provides ample additional suggestions.

Two of the best ways that children and young people gain information are to be found in the use of historic site education programs and oral history accounts of first-hand information from those who are "oldtimers" in the area. The local library and historical society should be basic sources of information about local history. Hofstra's Long Island Studies Institute has a wealth of photographs, maps, documents, and newspaper clippings, as well as extensive published materials.

Laura MacDermeid presented an outstanding "hands-on" program for elementary school children at the Huntington Historical Society. The children spent an entire day learning about children in earlier times through participation in their chores and pleasures. Information about the current program is contained in the epilogue at the end of her essay. Most larger historical societies and museums now offer educational programs for school visits.

When planning a field trip, it is always wise to preview the site and make certain that the setting is best for the group involved. Many historic sites have programs geared to different age groups. Taking students on a field trip to a site whose program is geared to an older age group may discourage future visits to the place, and not enhance the first experience. Unless the teacher is very knowledgeable, it is best to have the professionals at the site present the program.

Surely one of the most rewarding ways for students to develop a feeling for the recent past is by gathering oral history. Dr. Charles Howlett and his Advanced Placement classes at Amityville Memorial High School did this for a number of years, interviewing, reporting, and collating the information in a *Journal of Historical Inquiry.* For these young people to have the opportunity to talk with those who lived through the period being researched, whether it be the Depression or World War II or the post-war years, has made those times far more real and meaningful than merely reading about them in a textbook.

While Howlett's students were older, more skilled at questioning, and more sophisticated in synthesizing and presenting their material, this same oral history method has been used with elementary school children in the gifted and talented "Challenge" group in the Patchogue-Medford School District.

Their efforts are preserved in *The Patchwork Book,* copies of which can be found in the Long Island Studies Institute collection. Although these works were written by young people and children in advanced groups, collecting oral history and the use of primary sources can be done with almost any group under careful teacher supervision. *Farmingdale's Story, Farms to Flights* (originally written in 1956 and revised in a special Bicentennial edition in 1976) is a local history of Farmingdale, compiled by the Junior Historical Club in the local junior high school. Publications such as these, as well as the process of gathering the information, help students to "know the place" better than any textbook could hope to do.

Many older people who have grown up in the area are often delighted to be invited to speak to classes about their childhood: the clothing they wore, the games they played, the schooling they received, the appearance of the community in their youth. Retired teachers can bring a wealth of information about changes in education in the district and know how to speak to young people. Retired business or professional people and local government officials often are happy to talk about their former work. What better way to teach about the twentieth century than to give young people an opportunity to listen to those who have lived in it, allow an opportunity to ask questions and to receive answers. Local historical societies usually are able to suggest to newcomers the names of possible speakers. Recording the talks, questions and answers, and preserving them with an index or transcription, will enable future classes to learn firsthand about this century even after the oldtimers are gone. If this is not done, much of the social history of any given area will be lost forever.

Textbooks tend to focus on the "big" issues, e.g., origins and first settlers, wars, and events of national importance. But for children and young people to really develop a sense of place and an understanding of history, it is necessary for them to understand the everyday life of their area and its so-called "common" people. All too often the twentieth century is omitted entirely, with the excuse that there is a lack of time to teach it. Yet, the use of oral history, the visits to local historic houses and museums, and the backgrounds of local businesses, events or street names are of greater value for catching the students' interest and making history live in the minds of the next generation.

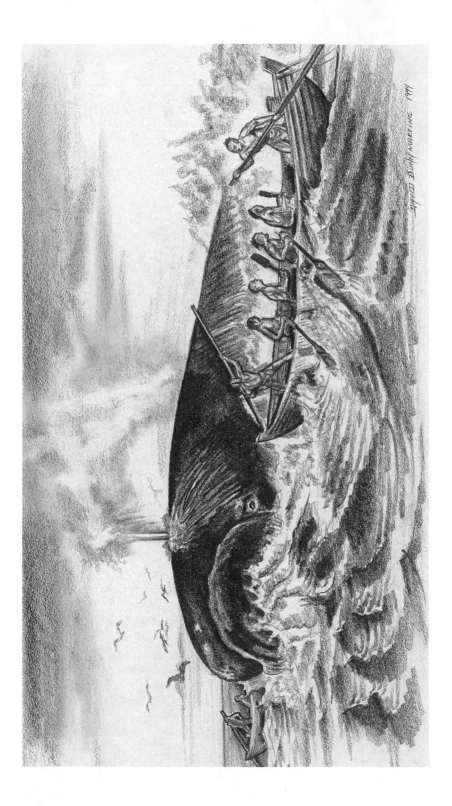

Indian Labor During the Post-Contact Period on Long Island, 1626–1700

John A. Strong

The cultural interactions between Indians and whites which followed the establishment of European settlements near aboriginal villages have been the subject of romantic folktales describing massacres, kidnapped Indian princesses, idyllic relations between heroic whites and noble Indian warriors, and "vanishing tribes" (Strong 1991: 253–8; Strong 1994; Strong and Karabag 1991: 191–3). Long Island historians writing in the nineteenth century repeated these fanciful accounts rather than analyzing the colonial documents for an understanding of the Indians' role in Long Island history. Unfortunately, textbooks currently in use in most Long Island schools draw heavily from these archaic sources (Strong 1994).

Over the last thirty years, anthropologists and historians have turned their attention to the relations between Indians and whites as the frontier moved westward from New England and Long Island. Several useful analytical models have emerged from these studies. Anthropologists Edward Spicer (1962: 519–39), Ralph Linton (1963: 463–520), and Robert Murphey (1964: 852–3) divided the post-contact period into two phases, "non-directed acculturation" and "directed acculturation." The non-directed acculturation phase is characterized by a free exchange of ideas and material goods and a voluntary adaptation of items and practices which do not change lifeways in any fundamental degree.[1] A more recent model, developed by Richard White (1983, 1991), describes this phase as a "middle ground," where two cultures meet on fairly even military terms, similar in many ways to the recent "cold war."

The two cultures met on the middle ground to trade, but the Indians found their sovereignty being gradually eroded. They were caught up in a process of directed acculturation where their aboriginal lifeways were changed under coercion: religious ceremonies prohibited, trade restricted, the choice of leaders manipulated by whites, and villages moved. Both individuals and whole tribes were entrapped in various forms of debt peonage.

These analytical categories are, of course, generalizations which can sometimes mislead. The Indians were not merely passive recipients of European policy. They struggled to protect their interests and their basic core values even as their political and military power was waning. A closer examination of the colonial records on Long Island suggests that, although the patterns of dependency and exploitation are the dominant theme, the Indians were often resourceful in manipulating a system stacked against them. They were also adept at selectively adapting aspects of European culture while maintaining their identity as Indians.

European Arrivals 1624–1650

The small group of about thirty families, who established New Netherland in 1624, began a very profitable fur trade which encouraged the Dutch to expand the colony and develop an extensive trade network reaching to Indian communities north along the Hudson and east to the Connecticut River Valley. The Dutch and their Indian trading partners met as equals on the middle ground for nearly two decades. As long as the Dutch activities were limited to a relatively small population of traders and administrative personnel, they posed no threat to the Indians.

By 1640, however, the Dutch colonial policy took a dramatic change in response to the growing threat from the English colonies in New England. The Dutch realized that they could not hold their colonial possessions unless they expanded their population base and fixed themselves more permanently on the land. Families were actively recruited to settle on farms and establish businesses in New Netherland. The new policy of agricultural colonization required more land and soon led to war with the neighboring Indian communities. Under the leadership of Governor Willem Kieft, the Dutch defeated the Indian resistance and expanded the Dutch settlements in what are now the boroughs of Brooklyn and Queens, and Nassau County.

At this same time, the English began to establish settlements on eastern Long Island. In December of 1640, about six months after the English settlers had arrived in Southampton, they negotiated a treaty endorsed by twelve Shinnecock Indians who were probably headmen from nearby villages (Strong 1983: 55, 67). The right to settle near their villages was granted in exchange for three-score bushels of corn, sixteen coats, and military protection. No attempt was made in the document to impose political authority over the Indians.

The first three decades of interaction were marked by a gradually increasing demand for European goods, which forced many Indians to seek employment with the whites. The aboriginal subsistence economy did not produce items which could be traded to the whites for such highly valued goods as guns, copper kettles, blankets, shoes, coats, and liquor. The request for corn in the 1640 treaty suggests that the Shinnecock did not produce an agricultural surplus which could be used for trade. Once the demand for wampum waned, the Indians had only two things of value to the whites: their land and their labor. The Indians entered the colonial labor market as whalers, free laborers, indentured servants, and slaves.

The Whaling Design

In October, as the arctic freeze reduces its food supply, the northern right whale *(Eubalena glacialis)* migrates south along the Atlantic coast to spawn in the warmer waters off the New England and Long Island shores. The whales remain in these waters until March when they return north. The right whales are vulnerable to hunters because they feed on the surface and swim close to the shore (Strong 1989: 29–30). Long before the arrival of the whites, Native Americans on Long Island and in southern New England had harvested beached whales and hunted sea mammals that came into the shallow coastal waters (Strong 1983: 32–4).

The potential profits from the sale of whale oil to London merchants prompted local entrepreneurs to combine Indian whaling skills with English technology.[2] Beginning around 1650, whaling companies were formed by settlers who hired Indian whalers and provided them with iron harpoons, thirty-foot cedar boats, and other tools necessary for hunting the whales and processing the oil from the blubber. During the next two decades, the owners paid the Indians with such trade goods as coats, cloth, boots, stockings, powder, shot, and alcohol. The bargaining power of the Indians and the importance of the whaling industry are underscored by the willingness of the colonial authorities to exempt whaling company owners from the laws prohibiting the sale of ammunition and alcohol to the Indians (NYCD 14: 608–9).

Most companies sent out two boats with six men on each: a harpooner, a steersman, and four oarsmen (Wooley 1968: 38–9). The average adult right whale is about fifty feet long and weighs one hundred tons, a formidable challenge to the Indians in their small boats. The harpooner had to cast his shaft into a moving target as the steersman and crew struggled to keep the boat close to the prey. The hunt could be over in an hour or so, if the lances hit a vital spot, but it was not unusual for the struggle to take half a day. After the kill, the long, exhaustive process of towing the whale to shore began (Strong 1989: 31).

The English were dependent on the Indians who had the skill and the courage to go out after the whales from November through March when the freezing waters meant death to those thrown from the small whale boats. The demand for skilled Indian whalers increased as the number of whaling companies grew. Company owners began to offer the Indian crews a half share of the blubber and bone and made liberal use of alcohol and other gifts in the negotiating process. Rival owners lured away whalers who had made commitments to other companies. In what appears to have been a response to this, the companies in Southampton, East Hampton, and Brookhaven drew up written contracts and recorded them with the town clerks. These contracts provide many important insights into the developing relationship between Indians and whites in the decades after the establishment of the English settlements.[3]

In 1687, the seven whaling companies operating out of Southampton and East Hampton produced 2,148 barrels of oil, valued from one and a half to two pounds sterling per barrel (Edwards and Rattray 1932: 201). Standards of measurement set by the colonial authorities required each barrel to contain thirty-one and one-half gallons. The gross income per company averaged about £700 sterling for the season. In order to appreciate the purchasing power of this income in the late seventeenth century, consider the following prices: farm land cost from £1 to £3 per acre (Kross 1983: 150–1, RTBH, Book B: 44); a herd of sixteen cows cost £64 (RTSH 2: 10); a horse cost £10; and the entire estate of John Stretton, Sr., one of the wealthiest men in East Hampton, was valued at £291 (DHNY 2: 441). By 1707, the companies had nearly doubled the number of barrels taken (Edwards and Rattray 1932: 202).

The whaling industry gave the Indians some economic power at first, but the English soon found ways to limit the impact of this advantage. English owners complained about the bargaining power of the Indians and appealed to the colonial government to place a cap on the wages paid to the Indian whalers. In 1672, Governor Lovelace complied by setting a limit of one-half share of the season's hunt to be divided up among the crew and a cloth coat for each whaler for every whale killed (NYCD 14: 675).[4] The Indians' share, however, was not paid to them in cash; it was "laid by" in the owners' hands as a credit line.[5]

The share or "lay" system of payment was very similar to the sharecropping system in the South during the late nineteenth and early twentieth centuries (Strong 1990: 19ff). Historian Daniel Vickers, who studied a similar lay system for Indian whalers on Nantucket, concluded that it was a form of debt peonage little different in principle from slavery (Vickers 1983: 583). Whaling contracts were usually negotiated at the end of the season in March or April for the next year. The whaler would then be able to purchase goods from the company owner on credit against the next season's share.

The owner would enter the value of the goods he gave each whaler in his account book. When the season ended, the total value of the whale oil and bone from the whales killed by the Indian crew would be determined by the company owner. The value of the goods taken on credit was also set by the owner, who would then calculate the cash value of the individual share for each crew member and deduct the amount owed him. This system enabled the owners to have the total income from the season's hunt, less only the cost of the goods which they sold, at a profit, to the Indians.

Two contracts negotiated in 1682 indicate that some of the Indian whalers suspected that the owners were inflating the prices of the goods extended in credit and reducing the cash value of the blubber in the Indian's share. Awonsis, Lenard, and Obadiah signed with James Hildreth with the stipulation that Hildreth charge them for the goods "at the same price as they can buy from others" (SHTA, Book D2: 87–8). Another crew, led by Wompy, Owanamako, Patumbum, and Panalsam, required the owner, Samuel Barnes, to pay them "as much as any other man will" for their share of the blubber (SHTA, Book D2: 107–8).

The whaling account book of William "Tangier" Smith, whose company operated out of Brookhaven from 1696 until 1721, provides detailed information about the nature of the lay system (Strong 1990: 17–28). None of the thirty-two Indian whalers who worked for Smith during those years ever got out of debt (Strong 1990: 22–3, table 6). A whaler named Abraham, who worked for eleven seasons, ended up ten pounds in debt to Smith. Another Indian named Sacutacca, who worked for ten seasons from 1697 to 1707, still owed Smith six pounds, six shillings, and eight pence. Many whalers found themselves so deeply in debt that they were forced to sign indentures for indefinite periods of time. One Shinnecock whaler named Artor, who had served several Southampton whaling companies from 1671 to 1679, owed so much money that "not knowing how to make satisfaction for the said debt" he agreed to indenture himself to John Fordham until the debt was paid (SHTA, Liber A: 133). Artor's case was not unique. Many of the whaling contracts signed from 1677 to 1685, included a clause obligating the Indians to continue working from season to season until their debts were paid off (RTEH 1: 407–9, 2: 78–9, 86–7, 152–3; SHTA, Book D2: 72, 87–8, 93, 99, 107–8, 112, 117–8, 127, 168, 172, 187).

The debt peonage system established in these contracts differs from the indentured servant system in one crucial aspect; it does not set a term limit on the labor commitment. The whaler lost his freedom to sell his labor on the open market for an undetermined length of time. When a Montauk whaler named Witness, who was in debt to Samuel Mulford of East Hampton, signed a contract to whale for John Wheeler, Mulford immediately protested that Witness was in debt to him and could not whale for anyone else until the debt was paid. Mulford entered his official protest into the record along with his own company contract which included Witness and three other Indian whalers (RTEH 2: 98–100).

Although the system was exploitive, the credit line with the company owners gave the whalers access to such highly valued European goods as powder, shot, cloth, coats, shoes, and alcohol. Undoubtedly they were accorded fairly high status in their own communities. Their own people probably saw them as great hunters in a traditional context rather than as exploited servants of the English. Six of the whalers were identified as sachems in their contracts: Wennahum of Shelter Island; Chice, Ponguamo, and Mahmanamon of Shinnecock; and Mousup and Wampanacomps of Montauk (RTSH 2: 68; SHTA, Liber A: 99, Book D2: 75, 168; RTEH 1: 407–9).

Indentured Servitude

The indenture system served several important functions in the colonial labor market. Although it is best known as a mechanism providing poor immigrants with a means of paying their passage to the colonies, the system provided a basic structure for the unskilled labor market. This market included Indians, African Americans, and poor whites who were born in the colonies. Town officials used the system to place paupers, orphans, and abandoned children with families who could afford to keep them as servants (Lott 1964: 125; Galenson 1981: 6–8; Jernegan 1931: 106; Seybolt 1917: 90). Occasionally parents in poor families would negotiate indentures for their children, which called for a cash payment upon signing the contract and a guarantee that the child would be properly fed and clothed, taught to read and write, and given training in a skilled trade.

Provisions for literacy and skills, however, were seldom included in the indentures for Indians and African Americans (Seybolt 1917: 89–90). One interesting exception to this pattern is an indenture negotiated between an Indian named Toby and Arthur Futhy, a carpenter in Brookhaven in 1684.[6] Toby agreed to work for a term of three years, during which he would serve his master by day and night and never leave his residence without permission.

The contract also listed, in rather demeaning terms, all the things that Toby should not do (RTBH, Book B: 191–2). He was not to steal from his master, nor to damage his goods, nor to allow them to be stolen or damaged by anyone else. Toby was admonished to keep his master's secrets and to behave in such a way that he himself would have nothing at all to hide. He was not to frequent taverns or ale houses nor to "play cards or dice or any unlawful game." The terms also included two very intrusive personal prohibitions. Toby was told that "matrimony he shall not contract, fornication he shall nott commit." These prohibitions are commonly found in seventeenth-century indentures, suggesting that the servants actually had a very lively social life which their masters sought, probably in vain, to curtail.[7]

In exchange for Toby's service, disciplined behavior, and silence, Arthur Futhy agreed to teach Toby the "art and mystery of a house carpenter soe far as he shall be capable to learn." Arthur also promised to provide room, board, and clothing. At the end of Toby's three-year term, Arthur would give him two new suits of apparel "from head to foot," one for working days and the other for holy days, one broad axe, one hand saw, one square, a pair of compasses, a broad and a narrow chisel, a gouge, an auger, and forty shillings. Toby's indenture was not at all typical for an Indian laborer. Few Indians ever got such an opportunity to learn a skilled trade.[8]

The earliest reference to an Indian servant on Long Island in the English colonial records provides some important social insights. In 1644, only four years after the settlement of Southampton was established, an Indian woman named Hope was a servant in the home of Edward Howell, a prominent Southampton settler. It seems likely that Hope came with the Howells from Massachusetts in 1640. She may have been one of the Pequot women taken prisoner in the devastating Pequot War.

Howell had another servant, a white man named George Wood, living in his household as well. Wood and Hope established a relationship which led to her pregnancy and created a scandal in the new settlement. The two were treated in accordance with the prevailing code of justice. They were forced to admit in a public court that they "consented to commit carnal filthiness together" and that George was the father (RTSH 1: 35). Then they were both humiliated further with a public whipping. The child was assigned to Edward Howell to be his indentured servant until the "basely begotton" child reached the age of thirty.

Hope is one of the few Indian servant women mentioned in the colonial records. She is mentioned, of course, because of the scandal, but most of the entries refer to men. Several of the indentures in the East Hampton town records involve Indian whalers and their families. One of the earliest of these contracts, signed in 1678, bound an Indian named Tom to the Reverend Thomas James for the term of three and a half years. The contract was witnessed by Tom's brother, Abel, who went to sea for James' whaling company in 1677 (RTEH 2: 407–9).

Tom was obligated to serve the clergyman for three and a half years and to do him "faithful service and to be obedient to all his lawful commands by day or night," in return for which James promised to "allow the said Tom meate drinke and clothing sufficient for him, and a coate a year . . . and when his three years and a half is out to leave him as well clothed as I find him and two coates of Trucking cloth" (RTEH 1: 410). Tom had been indentured to another settler named Roger Smith prior to his contract with James. Tom's indenture, which is typical of the Indian indentures, stands in sharp contrast to Toby's contract. Tom got two coats, no other clothes, no training, and no tools for the same term of service.

The specific terms of the indentures varied widely. John Indian, a Montauk, bound himself out to Richard Stretton of East Hampton for a two year term in 1683. John was to receive twelve pounds at the end of the term. If he went out on a whaling expedition, however, he was to receive his half share in addition to the twelve pounds payment (RTEH 2: 132–3). John Mahue, also a Montauk, indentured himself to Philip Leake of East Hampton for three months and was paid only three pounds, six shillings, about half the monthly rate paid to John Indian. Jeffrey, another Montauk Indian, bound himself out to Richard Shaw for a term of seven years for a payment of twenty pounds, less than three pounds a year, and room and board (RTEH 2: 212).

In some instances, parents who negotiated indentures for their young children received a few shillings when the contract was signed. Two such contracts were negotiated by a veteran Montauk whaler named Papasequin, for his son and daughter. Papasequin's name appears on eight whaling contracts between 1675 and 1683 (RTEH 2: 78–9, 86–7, 95–6, 373–4; SHTA, Liber A: 90; SHTA, Book D2: 74, 85, 117–8). In 1685, Papasequin and his wife bound out their seven-year-old son, Quansurh, to Jacob Schellinger for a ten year term beginning in 1688 (RTEH 2: 173). Papasequin, who had gone to sea for Schellinger in 1679, may have wanted his son to become a whaler. Schellinger paid Papasequin twenty shillings when the child was delivered to him in 1688 and ten pounds to Quansurh at the end of his term.

Six years later Papasequin and his wife bound out their daughter, Marget, to Daniel Osborn for a seven year term (EHTA, 10 WB, 126). Osborn paid the parents three pounds and gave their daughter room and board and three pounds when she finished her term. Both children undoubtedly experienced a rather dramatic immersion in English culture and values, but there was no provision for teaching them English or preparing them for a trade.

Jerred, an Indian servant to John Youngs of Southold, bequeathed his six-year-old son, Young Jerred, to his master in 1678 (RTS 1: 154). Jerred, who was dying of consumption, indentured his son to Youngs for nineteen years. There was no mention in the agreement of any payment to either Jerred or to his son when the term was completed. Not all children had parents who could represent them in negotiating their indenture. A one-year-old Montauk orphan, named Hopewell, was indentured by his Indian guardians to John Fixthand, an East Hampton man, for a twenty-five year term. When the child was six, Fixthand sold the remaining nineteen years of the indenture to the Reverend Thomas James for fifteen pounds sterling (EHTA, Leather Bound Book: 34). James agreed to pay Hopewell ten pounds at the end of his nineteen-year term and give him a suit of clothes. Fixthand made more on the transaction than Hopewell made for his long years of labor.

Hopewell's experience raises another unpleasant aspect of the indenture system. Servants, like slaves, could be bought and sold without their consent. They could also be leased or "rented out" by their masters. An Indian named Adso, for example, who had signed a contract with John Miller, Jr. of East Hampton for two whaling seasons beginning in 1684, was sent by Miller to whale for Richard Shaw on December 11, 1684 (RTEH 2: 152–3).

In contrast to the Indian indentures, the bonds for whites were more likely to include a clause requiring the children to be taught a trade and basic reading and writing skills (Seybolt 1917: 91). In 1683, for example, Renock Garrison bound out his six-year-old son Samuel to Isaack and Elizabeth Mills until he reached his twenty-fifth birthday (RTHE 2: 133). The boy was to be trained as a carpenter and taught to read and write. The Garrisons also bound out two other children, John (aged twelve) and Anna (aged three), to be apprenticed to a weaver. These children also were to receive reading and writing instruction. The difference is significant because it clearly indicates that the Indians were viewed as a permanent underclass who would provide domestic and unskilled labor for the English.

Indian Slavery

Some Indians were slaves who served for life and were chattel in the eyes of the law. Unfortunately, the data relating to Indian slavery in colonial America is very sparse (Lauber 1913: 105–17). The primary source of Indian slaves in southern New England and on Long Island were the captives from the Pequot War (1637) and King Philip's War (1675–1676). A small number of Indian slaves also were imported from the Carolinas and from the Spanish colonies. Indian captives were usually sold into slavery in some distant port, because they could easily escape to a friendly refuge if they remained near their own people.

Some Indians were enslaved by court order as a penalty for a crime, but these were usually shipped to the West Indies or Bermuda (Lauber 1913: 201). Nangenutch, a Montauk Indian found guilty of attempted rape, was sentenced to be whipped and sold into slavery in the West Indies in 1668 (Strong 1994). Nangenutch, however, broke out of jail and was not recaptured.

One of the Indian slaves who came to Long Island in the slave trade was a young girl named Beck. In 1677, James Loper purchased Beck from Samuel Rogers, who lived in New England. Beck, who is identified in the document as a "captive," was probably captured by English troops during King Philip's War. She was purchased, said Loper, to help his wife with her household chores. According to the bill of sale, Loper was "to hould possess and enjoy his ... proper estate during her natural life" (RTEH 1: 412–3).

Indian slavery was abolished by the colonial government in 1679, when it ordered that all Indians were to be free except for those who had been imported into the colony and sold here (NYCD 13: 537–8). These "foreign" Indian slaves brought into the colony had to be exported within six months or they would be freed. The six month period was apparently granted to allow a slave trader to sell the Indian slaves to a buyer who would take the Indians out of New York. The law was not enforced because there are many references to Indian slaves both in New York and on Long Island until all slavery was ended in 1827. Complaints were made to Governor Clinton as late as 1750, that Indian children born in New York were being sold as slaves (Lauber 1913: 200).

In 1687, Thomas Hawarden of New York City sold an Indian slave named Will to Christopher Dene in Hempstead. The boy was to belong to Dene "forever." Hawarden said that he was "legally seized of the said Indian boy as his own proper slave and hath full power and legal authority to sell and dispose of the same to the said Christopher Dene" (RTNSH 2: 60). Hawarden had apparently purchased Will in New York City from a slave dealer. There is no indication in the records that Dene's purchase was ever challenged by the colonial authorities. Shortly thereafter Dene sold the boy to Nathaniel Prime (Moss 1993: 11).

In 1688, the colonial government had ruled that all Indian slaves brought into New York who could prove that they were Christian subjects of the King of Spain and could say the Lord's Prayer were to be set free at once and returned to their homes (Lauber 1913: 317). The recitation of the Lord's Prayer was apparently a test to make sure that the Indians had been Christians prior to their enslavement. The 1665 Duke's Laws and later legislation made it clear that slaves could not gain their freedom by converting to Christianity.

Indian slaves were listed in wills and estate records long after the 1679 emancipation order was issued. In Newtown, Long Island, just across the river from Manhattan, three Indian slaves were listed in the estate records. In 1691, Jonathan Strickland, a resident of Newtown, listed an Indian slave boy in his estate and valued him at ten pounds sterling. Four decades later, William Parcell left his daughter an Indian woman and a young boy in his will (Kross 1983: 92). William Smith, patriarch of St. George's Manor in Brookhaven, bequeathed Negro and Indian slaves to his children in 1704. In 1724, Arent Schuyler of New York left two Indian slave women to his daughters (Lauber 1913: 114).

Private citizens ignored the law, and public officials apparently cooperated in the return of Indian slaves who tried to escape illegal captivity. Advertisements were run in the Manhattan newspapers identifying runaway Indian slaves. In July 1733, the *New York Gazette* advertised for the return of a runaway Indian slave from Flushing, Long Island. In the February 6–13, 1739 edition of the *Gazette*, Moses Gombauld, a merchant, asked for the return of an eighteen-year-old Indian slave boy who spoke French, English, and Spanish. Later that same year, William Sims announced that his slave, a twenty-five-year-old Indian, had run away. The Indian had previously been owned by Obediah Smith of Smithtown (McKee 1935: 115). Similar advertisements were run in the *New York*

Weekly Mercury in 1740 and 1756, for Indian slaves from New York and Long Island (Lauber 1913: 115).

In one case, however, a courageous Indian slave woman named Sarah, "the daughter of Dorkas, an Indian woman" did raise a challenge in her own behalf. Sarah had been sold to John Parker of Southampton for sixteen pounds by James Parshall when she was only eight years old (Adams 1918: 120). According to the entry in the town record, Sarah became Parker's property "during her natural life." In 1712, when she was twenty-three, Parker sold her and an Indian boy named Abel to John Wick of Bridgehampton for twenty-one pounds, twelve shillings. Wick sold Sarah to a merchant in New York who took her to the island of Madeira to be sold in the slave market there.

Sarah, with a surprising display of resourcefulness given her circumstances, petitioned the English consul on the island and claimed that she was born of free Indian parents. She further charged that neither Parker nor Wick held a valid title of ownership and asked that they be challenged to produce proof of their claims. The consul granted her request and arranged for her return, but there is no record of what happened to Sarah after that.

Sarah's claim that she was born of free Indian parents raised an important legal issue because the colony had enacted a law in 1707, which stated that "all and every Negro, Indian, Mulatto and Mestee Bastard child and children who are and shall be born of any Negro, Indian, Mulatto or Mestee shall follow ye state and condition of the mother and he be esteemed reputed taken and adjudged a slave to all intents and purposes whatsoever" (Lincoln 1894: 598). The children of free Indian men and African-American slave mothers, therefore, became slaves because of their mother's status. Sarah probably had this statute in mind when she testified that her mother, Dorkas, had been free.

The increasing number of references to "mustees" and "mulattos" in the early eighteenth century records probably refer to these children. Although many of these "mustees" were as much Indian as they were African American, the whites categorized them into a lower socio-economic status, denying them their "Indianness." This arbitrary racial classification was romanticized by the whites who "lamented the vanishing Indians."

The relationship between Indian and African American slaves and servants is not surprising. They suffered much the same exploitation, and they shared the same servant's quarters in the English households. In a few instances they joined together in violent revolt against their masters. In 1657, when several buildings in Southampton were burned by Indian servants, troops had to be sent from Connecticut to investigate and restore order. Wyandanch, the Montauk sachem who was a close ally of the English, testified that "a mischievous Negar woman servant . . . [was] fare deeper in that capital miscarriage then any or all of the Indians" (RCNP 10: 180). Unfortunately, no other records of this intriguing event have survived, so we can not corroborate Wyandanch's testimony. If the sachem's account is true, it would certainly be interesting to hear what the woman's grievance was and how she managed to have such influence over her Shinnecock co-conspirators.

A much more serious revolt involving African-American and Indian slaves took place in New York City in 1712 (Scott 1961). The roots of the revolt have been traced back to an incident in Newtown, Long Island, which is reminiscent of Wyandanch's account above. On January 24, 1708, an Indian slave named Sam was encouraged by an African-American slave woman to kill their owner and his family.[9] The two slaves and their two African-American accomplices were arrested, tried, and executed ten days later. The woman was burned at the stake, Sam was hung, and the two other men were tortured to death (Scott 1961: 45).

Many African American and Indian slaves were outraged at the cruelty of the executions, and their anger smoldered for four years. On New Year's day, 1712, a small cadre of about fifty Indians and African American slaves did launch a plot to kill all of the whites in New York City (Scott 1961: 46). An African American slave named Cuffee and an Indian slave named John set a diversionary fire to attract the whites, who rushed to put it out. As the whites arrived, they were attacked by the small band of slaves. Eight white men were killed and twelve more were wounded.

The slaves fled, but the militia soon hunted them down. Six of the men killed themselves as the troops approached. Only four of the slaves were identified as Indians, but it is likely that there were more. Two of the Indians, John and Hosea, were from the

Spanish colonies, and the others, Ambrose and Tom, were probably brought in by the slave trade as well. Ambrose and Tom were acquitted, but John and Hosea were found guilty and sentenced to hang. Both, however, were later pardoned by the governor.

The Indian slaves may have been treated more leniently than the Africans because their legal status was ambiguous. The governor noted that John and Hosea, who had been imported from the Spanish colonies about 1705, had petitioned him before the incident, claiming that they had been kidnapped and sold into slavery by pirates. Governor Hunter said that he had not freed them because the Indians could not produce any written documents to substantiate their claim. This requirement, of course, was an impossible task for Hosea and John.

This procedure may explain, in part, why so many Indians remained slaves so long after the 1679 emancipation order. By placing the burden of proof on the Indians, the New York officials virtually guaranteed that the owner's claim would prevail. The governor makes no mention of the clause in the 1680 law which called for the freeing of any Indian slave who remained in the colony for more than six months.

In 1750, Governor Clinton ordered that all Indian children born of free parents who were still held as slaves be returned to their parents. In spite of the governor's order, there were still isolated instances of Indian slavery on Long Island for several years (Lauber 1913: 201). All of the Indian slaves, including those who were imported in the slave trade, were finally freed along with the African American slaves in 1827.

Indian Free Labor

Not all Indians entered the English economic system as slaves or indentured servants. Free laborers were hired for the day or for a specific job and were paid upon completion of the task in money or in goods. Many Indians worked on a part-time basis for English farmers, merchants, and artisans. Some of these jobs, such as fence watching, tending livestock, rescuing livestock from wetland swamps, carrying flour from the mill to the homes, and doing chores around the farm, did not require much skill, but a few tasks, such as the construction of rail fences, guiding hunters and fishermen, and the trying of whale oil were skilled crafts. Indians brought meat and tanned hides from game

animals, fish, and shellfish which they had caught or dug, and feathers they had collected which they sold or traded for English manufactured goods. They also made goods such as scrub brushes and baskets for sale or trade. By the beginning of the eighteenth century, many Montauk were raising livestock of their own. They recorded the earmarks of their cattle, swine, and horses in the town records along with the English farmers' marks (RTEH 3: 134, 170, 186–7, 271, 317, 423; 4: 9, 124). Most of the food from these animals, however, was consumed by the owners rather than sold for a profit.

Many Indians were attracted to the English towns where they could find odd jobs. Nangenutch, the young Montauk who was accused of molesting three different English women in East Hampton, had been hired to carry sacks of flour from the mill to the kitchens where the alleged molestations occurred (Strong 1994). The young Montauk had previously been employed as a servant to Richard Shaw of East Hampton. There were undoubtedly many Indians who did odd jobs in the colonial settlements throughout Long Island, but the incidents of sexual contact were much more likely to involve English masters and Indian servant women.[10]

We know of Nangenutch's work because of the sensational trial, but most of the information about unskilled labor is limited to brief references in public and private account books. An entry in the East Hampton Trustees Journal, for example, authorized the payment of nine pence to Montauks who brought them information about livestock mired in the swamps or about dead animals whose skin was still salvageable. If the Indians rescued an animal, they would be paid eighteen pence (RTEH 1: 137).

In the spring of 1698, the town of East Hampton paid two Montauk Indians, Ben and Pharaoh, seven shillings, six pence for repairing and maintaining the fence around the grazing fields at Montauk for the summer (RTEH 2: 392). The average daily pay for unskilled labor in the latter half of the seventeenth and early eighteenth centuries was three shillings (RTEH 2: 220, RTSH 5: 5; Kross 1983: 134). Even if we assume that Ben and Pharaoh were not on duty every day all summer, the pay is well below the daily rate for an English worker.

That same spring, Weomp, a veteran Montauk whaler who had gone to sea for three different East Hampton whaling companies as a young man (1675–1681),[11] was given one pound sterling, "as part pay for Ginning'" (RTEH 2: 392). "Gin," derived from the preindustrial word for "engine" meaning a device of some sort, was used in the eighteenth century to describe a trap or enclosure for livestock. The animals were driven into the gin before they were moved from the summer grazing areas to the winter fields so that they could be counted. The ear marks on each animal identified the owners who were then charged for the grazing rights. Weomp was paid much more than Ben and Pharaoh, perhaps, because the ginning required more skill and responsibility.[12]

Some of these labor contracts included a clause setting a bond obligation guaranteeing completion of the assigned tasks. When Hanable, an Indian from Shelter Island, signed an agreement on March 5, 1698, to search the woods and wetlands for Nathaniel Sylvester's cattle over a six week period, he agreed to pay his employer ten pounds sterling if he failed to find all of the livestock. Hanable was to be paid two pounds sterling in advance and two more at the end of his term."[13] He would earn about three shillings a day, but he also ran the risk of assuming a debt that was more than twice his salary for six weeks labor.

Few of the other domestic servants and unskilled day workers are mentioned in the colonial documents unless they are mentioned in written contracts. One such contract was negotiated in December 1679, between Thomas Biggs, Jr. of Brookhaven and Gie (Guy), a sachem from Setauket. Gie agreed to clear five acres of land for Biggs, cutting down all of the little trees, "that is about as big as ones leg" (RTBH, Book B: 28). In return Biggs was to pay the sachem four pounds, ten shillings if the work was completed in time for the spring planting in May. If the work was not finished until the fall, Gie would be paid four pounds in trading cloth at ten shillings per yard. Gie was given one coat when the contract was signed and a second coat when the task was finished.

Another of the unskilled jobs which was important enough to the English to require written contracts was fence minding on Montauk. An agreement between the Montauk and the Town of East Hampton, signed in 1655, allowed the settlers to graze their livestock in the Indians' planting grounds after the fall harvest until the spring planting in late April or early May. The settlers agreed to construct fences that would keep their animals from the Indians' crops during the summer growing season.

Fences needed constant watching. Even those built "pig tight, horse high and bull strong" were often weakened by the weather and the constant probing of the livestock. The town of East Hampton hired Montauk Indians to monitor the fences, day and night, from April to October. The Indians were asked to set up their wigwams just inside the fences and to live there for the season. The timing was perfect for whalers, because their season was finished by April. The Indians were paid by a barter system rather than in cash.

In April 1683, for example, Quaquehide (Harry) was hired to watch the Montauk fence and, in return, the town would arrange to have an acre of land plowed near his wigwam and give him ten bushels of corn (RTEH 2: 125–6). The town paid ten shillings to have the acre plowed and four shillings a bushel for the corn (RTEH 2: 393; 3: 143). The total value of the goods and services, therefore, was two pounds, ten shillings. Quaquehide would be finished with his fence duties in time to go to whaling in November. The following year another whaler, named Jeffrey, and his wife were hired under a similar arrangement, except that the couple received a coat in addition to the plowing and the corn (RTEH 2: 145–6).

Fences, of course, play a vital role in any agricultural system. There were serious legal consequences for any farmer who did not keep his fences in good repair. If his livestock got out because his fences were allowed to fall into disrepair, he would be liable for any damage they caused. Fence construction, therefore, was a highly valued skill. Indians who were accustomed to working with the wood from local trees were often recruited and trained in the use of iron woodworking tools.

In November 1681, Gie, the Setauket sachem who had cleared the land for Thomas Biggs, was hired by John Roe to construct a post-and-rail fence five rails high at eighteen pence a rail (RTBH, Book B: 509). The fence had to be completed for the spring planting in April. Gie was to be assisted by an Indian named Gudger, who also worked as a whaler (RTBH, Book B: 105). This New England-style fence, unlike the postless split rail "zig-zag" fences in the southern colonies, required considerable skill. The six-foot long posts were cut from foot-thick chestnut or cedar trees and split in half. A hole was then chiseled every four to six inches in the upper portion of the post. Eleven-foot long rails were cut from oak or ash trees and fitted into the holes in the posts (Hawke 1988: 35).

Two Indians, Arastottle and Cellis (Kellis), signed a similar fence contract with John Tooker, Jr. of Brookhaven in May 1683 (RTBH, Book B: 148–9). Arastottle was to cut two hundred eleven-foot rails and seven five-hole posts and have them ready in three weeks. Kellis agreed to cut sixty more five-hole posts in one month's time. The contract does not mention the payment for the two men. It is possible that Arastottle and Kellis were working to pay off a previous debt. This was the case in another fence contract in 1685, between Jeremy and Bumbrest and a Brookhaven man named Arthur Futhy. The two Indians agreed to cut six hundred split rails and to have them ready for carting in six weeks (RTBH, Book B: 242–3). In return, Futhy was to pay Adam Smith one pound, thirteen shillings and John Thomas six shillings. Apparently these were debts owed by the Indians to the Englishmen. Jeremy and Bumbrest did receive six shillings when they signed the contract. Jeremy, like Gudger and several other Indians, had a second job. He had gone whaling for Andrew Gibb of Brookhaven in 1682 (RTBH, Book B: 105).

If the Indian workers did not meet the deadlines set in the contracts, they could be hauled into court and sued by their employer. When Bumbrest was unable to deliver the rails on time, Futhy took Bumbrest to court and forced him to cut an extra one hundred rails as a penalty (RTBH, Book B: 254). The Indian also had to give Futhy six days of labor and pay the court costs.

That same day in court, John Tooker, Jr. also sued Bumbrest along with Kellis, who had worked for Tooker in 1683. The court ruled that the Indians, "having made an agreement with John Tooker for a certain parcel of fencing akording to the writing between them and they not doing of it akording to time, therefore they both of them agree to give the abovesaid John Tooker twenty shillings and pay court charges." The two Indians were thereby forced out of the free labor market and trapped in a cycle of debt peonage.

Another important task requiring specific skills was the processing (trying) of the whale oil. Although most whaling companies expected the whaling crews to process the blubber into marketable oil, some owners negotiated individual contracts with Indians to carry out this arduous task. The cutting was done on the beach after the whale had been towed ashore and anchored at the tide line. Using a hawser and tackle, the strips of blubber were peeled off in a process which often took several days (Edwards and Rattray 1932: 90–6). The blubber was cut into large chunks, loaded onto carts, and taken to the nearest trying station.

At the station, the chunks of blubber were minced into thin slices and placed in 250 gallon copper kettles on top of a brick fireplace. As the oil was boiled out of the blubber, it was skimmed off and poured into a cooling kettle. The boiled-out meat scraps were fished out and used to fuel the fire. As the oil cooled, it was transferred to wooden barrels. The whole operation could take as long as a week if the whale was a large adult.

In 1680, Jonathan Hildreth and John Carwithy hired Sequanah, who was probably Shinnecock, to try the blubber from the season's hunt. Hildreth and Carwithy provided the pots and the wood for the fire. Sequannah was to be paid two shillings six pence per barrel, "or that which is equivalent." The last clause suggests that he might be paid in goods or credit rather than in cash (RTSH 2: 80). The following year Weeis and Masagandsag, negotiated a better rate, three shillings six pence from Thomas Cooper and Samuel Barnes, but they had to agree to pay for any oil that was lost because of their negligence (SHTA, Book D2: 71).

Apparently the rate of two shillings six pence was generally accepted because two other contracts, one in 1682 and a second in 1683, were set at that rate (SHTA, Book D2: 84, 131). Gie, the Setauket sachem, and an Indian named Towaring were hired by

Andrew Gibb at that rate as well, but Gibb added a bonus of two bushels of corn (RTBH, Book B: 109).

Conclusion

The colonial documents used in this study clearly indicate that the Indians of Long Island passed through the "non-directed" phase of their post contact experience during the latter half of the seventeenth century and became increasingly dependent on the English market system. The desire for English manufactured goods gradually entrapped more and more Indians in a web of debt.

One indication of this growing dependency was the increasing pattern of adopting English names. In the first deeds to land in Southampton and East Hampton, there were no Indians using English names, and two decades later, only three of the twenty-four Indians who signed the February 1666 deed to Quogue had English names. By 1698, when the Southampton census was taken, over half of the Shinnecock had taken English first names (Strong 1983: 80–3). The adoption of these names, of course, was a matter of convenience for Indians who wished to deal with the whites. It was common for an Indian to carry two names during this period, one to use at home and the other for business with the settlers. In one of the East Hampton whaling contracts, for example, Montauk names are followed by "aliases" (RTEH 1: 407–9):

Towis	alias	Ben
Tantaquin	alias	Will
Jumpaus	alias	Nat
Quequecum	alias	Hector
Quaquehide	alias	Harry
Wunnanaugema	alias	Anthony
Wompaquat	alias	Haines
Sauan	alias	George

By the end of the eighteenth century all of the Indians listed in the public documents were using English names.

Even though the Montauk, Matinnecock, Shinnecock, and Poospatuck became more and more involved in the English economic structure, yet they retained their own identity as Indians. Although they became dependent on the outside economy and were given little chance to advance in status because of local prejudices, they did maintain a separate cultural tradition which continues to distinguish them from other ethnic groups. Their culture survives in their kinship systems, in their communal rites of passage and intensification, and in their folklore (Strong 1994). The task of defining Long Island Indian culture as it developed in the nineteenth and twentieth centuries is beyond the scope of this essay. It should be noted, however, that since World War II, more and more Indian young people have gone on to college to develop their potential. Many have returned to provide leadership that combines the strength of their traditions with their modern skills.

Notes

1. Mary Helms, an anthropologist who studied the relations between the Spanish colonizers in Nicaragua and the Miskito Indian communities, found the Miskito people had managed to maintain a non-directed relationship until recent times. They became, she argued, "purchase societies" existing on the margins of the Spanish economic, political, and social structures (Helms 1969, 1971).

2. Profits from whale oil were a major source of capital for the eastern towns on Long Island in the late seventeenth and early eighteenth centuries (Strong 1989: 30). Shortly after the first English settlement on eastern Long Island was established at Southampton in 1640, the settlers organized squads to cut the blubber from beached whales and "try" (boil) it into oil. The oil was then skimmed off and put into barrels which could be sold to merchants in Boston.

Individuals and towns vied for control of the rights to the beached whales. In 1658, Lion Gardiner and the Reverend Thomas James purchased the rights to beached whales from the eastern boundary of East Hampton to Montauk Point from Wyandanch, the Montauk sachem (RTEH 1: 150). The towns of East Hampton and Southampton, of course, assumed the whale rights on all beaches in their boundaries. Whaling rights to the beaches west of the original Southampton purchase from present day Canoe Place to Eastport were fought over in court for three decades. Lion Gardiner purchased whale rights to this area from Wyandanch and sold them to John Cooper and John Ogden. Both the Shinnecock and the Unkechaug (Poospatuck) sachems protested Wyandanch's authority to sell these rights, and the Setauket settlers agreed. The uncertainty over rights to this stretch of beach also led to many court battles over the rights to whale carcasses. It even turned brother against brother as John Cooper sued his brother, Thomas, for taking a whale from his beach (RTSH 2: 27–8).

3. Although the research is not completed, the author has located ninety-two whaling contracts recorded in the town records for Brookhaven, East Hampton, and Southampton between 1670 and 1685. The practice was abandoned after 1685, perhaps because the town officials could not, or were unwilling to, enforce them. The

owners, of course, kept their own account books, but few have survived. Fortunately, William "Tangier" Smith's "Pigskin Book," which includes his whaling contracts from 1696 to 1721, has been preserved by the Bellport-Brookhaven Historical Society (Strong 1990: 17–8).

These contracts list nearly 300 Indian names, and some identify them by tribe or location. It is impossible to give an exact number for the Indian signatures (signs) because several Indians took the same Christian first name such as John, Tom, Harry, or Ben. Another problem is posed by the use of phonetic spellings for the Indian names. The English clerks often spelled the same name two different ways in the same document. The Indian names themselves are a problem as well because Indians frequently took new names in response to an important event in their lives or a dream or vision. In spite of these difficulties, the data is very useful in determining patterns of acculturation.

4. The contracts failed to prevent the continual "jumping" by Indian whalers who were apparently attempting to negate the advantage gained by the owners in the wage cap. John Topping petitioned Governor Andros at the beginning of the whaling season in December 1680, complaining that the owners were "much disappointed and damnified in their business of whaling by the deceits and unfaithfulness of the Indians" who had been signed to a contract the previous spring with one owner, received some goods for signing, and then later in the summer signed again with another owner (NYCD 14: 756–7). The Indians, continued Topping, "having received goods of one man in the spring upon account of whaling and now again of another to fit them for the sea leave their masters to quarrel." Topping asked that the town constables and overseers in the eastern towns intervene and stop the abuses. There is no record of any action taken by the governor.

The colonial government did pass a law in 1708, which was designed to make sure that there were whalers available for hire during the season. Apparently there was such a limited supply of experienced Indian whalers in relation to the demand that unusual efforts had to be taken. The law stated that all Indians under contract to whaling companies "shall not at any time or times between the first day of November and the fifteenth day of April following yearly be sued, arrested, molested, detained, or kept out of that employment by any person or persons whatsoever" (Lincoln 1894: 610). If a company owner had a contract with a whaler, however, he could prevent the man from going to sea with any other company.

The same law also prohibited anyone from purchasing the goods given to a whaler in advance for signing a contract or for entertaining a whaler with alcohol "when they should be at sea or other business belonging to that design of whale fishing." The law was renewed in 1716 with no modifications.

5. In my article "From Hunter to Servant" in the 1985 edition of this publication, I stated that the whaling contracts which called for the Indian whalers to receive a half share of the blubber and bone,

brought them into the English cash economy. I assumed that the Indians sold their share for cash which they used to purchase trade goods. The Unkechaug Indians in Brookhaven did petition the governor to allow them to sell their blubber "to whom they liked best" (NYCD 14: 720), but subsequent research in the seventeenth century whaling records of Nantucket, Martha's Vineyard, and in William "Tangier" Smith's account book (the Pigskin Book in the Bellport Museum), indicates the "lay system" was the more common practice.

6. This may have been the same Toby who went to sea for Benjamin Conkling in 1681 (RTEH 2: 95–6) and is listed in the 1698 Southampton census (Strong 1983: 102–3). It is possible, of course, that there was more than one Indian named Toby on the eastern end of Long Island.

7. In the eighteenth century, printed forms were used for indentures which included all of the same prohibitions against marriage, fornication, drinking, and cards (HTHA: Indenture file; Seybolt 1917: 88).

8. A year earlier, for example, an Indian named Humphrey (Mahcarack) signed an indenture with Andrew Gibb of Brookhaven for a two-year term which included the same restrictions. Gibb paid off Humphrey's eleven pound debt to Richard Woodhall, but the Indian received no money and no training. He was provided with room and board and a coat at the end of his term (RTBH, Book B: 172–3).

9. There had been earlier signs of racial tensions. In 1706 Governor Cornbury "informed that several negroes in Kings county have assembled themselves in a riotous manner," ordered that all African Americans who have run away from their masters be arrested. If any resisted, the militia was ordered "to fire on them, kill, or destroy them" (Ostrander 1894, l: 171–2). The following year another alarm was sounded; this time the threat was from Long Island Indians who were reported to have plans to "destory the whites" (BHM: 353-4).

The New York authorities ordered the Long Island militias to be ready to march against the Indians. Unfortunately, there do not appear to be any other references in the surviving colonial records about these incidents.

10. In the Hempstead Town Records (RTNSH 1: 372), there is a brief entry which suggests that Joseph Jennings and an Indian woman named Mogrub had a son named Keewaquna. "Jos Jennings child was born May 16 1665 for the clockes His name is Keewaquna. Mogrub informs against him." It is possible that Mogrub wanted child support from Jennings. Bernice Marshall (1962: 50), in her history *Colonial Hempstead*, quotes this document and adds that the "parish records" included many such petitions. Unfortunately, Marshall did not provide a complete enough citation for the Town Clerk to locate them when this author attempted to examine them.

John Lyon Gardiner, the seventh lord of the manor on Gardiner's Island, was curious about rumors that his grandfather, John Gardiner, the third lord of the manor was the father of a Montauk woman named Betty Fowler. In his Journal and Farm Book (EHTA), John Lyon recounts a conversation he had on February 10, 1801, with George Pharaoh, an elderly Montauk Indian, about a Montauk woman named Betty Fowler, who was reputed to be John's daughter. Pharaoh told John Lyon that "old Mr. John" spoke Algonquian and "came to their wigwams to eat fresh fish and he liked the young squaws of the old sachem breed" (Gardiner, Farm Book, 157–8). Betty Fowler's daughter Mary was the wife of Samson Occom.

11. Although the spellings vary slightly on the whaling contracts (Weomp, Weaump, Weeump, Wemup), they are probably the same person. Weomp went to sea for Thomas James in 1675 (RTEH 1: 382), John Wheeler in 1680 (RTEH 2: 86–7), and Benjamin Conkling in 1681 (RTEH 2: 95–6). Weomp also signed the 1703 treaty which endorsed the 1687 sale of the last of the Montauk land to East Hampton and gave the Montauk residence rights at Montauk forever (MID, Folders 12, 13).

12. The following year Weomp was again paid one pound for "Jinning" (RTEH 2: 396). Two other Montauk, Will and Wittonees, were listed in the same document for "Mending and maintaining" the Montauk fence. Will was paid one pound, two shillings, and six pence in 1700, and Wittonees was paid three shillings in 1696.

13. This document is located in the Harry B. Sleight Collection (S.14) in the John Jermain Library, Sag Harbor, NY. The monetary term used in this document is "rials," a gold coin introduced by Edward IV in 1465, which was still in use in the early eighteenth century. A rial was originally worth about ten shillings according to the *Compact Edition of the Oxford English Dictionary*. This currency, rarely mentioned in seventeenth century Long Island documents, may have had a different value in 1689, but is is unlikely that Hanable would have been paid more than three shillings per day.

References

Primary Sources

BHM. 1866. ed. E. B. O'Callaghan. *Calendar of British Historical Manuscripts in the Office of the Secretary of State, Albany, NY, 1664–1776* British Historical Manuscripts, Office of the Secretary of State, Albany, NY: 52: 61–4, abstracted [Albany: Weed, Parsons and Company, 1866: 353–54]).

DHNY. 1849. *Documentary History of New York*, ed. E. B. O'Callaghan. 4 vols. Albany: Weed, Parsons, and Sons.

EHTA. East Hampton [Town] Archives, Long Island Room, East Hampton Public Library, East Hampton, NY.

EHTJ. *East Hampton Trustees Journal*. 7 vols. East Hampton: Town of East Hampton.

Gardiner, J. L. Journal and Farm Book, East Hampton Library Archives, Collection no. KA 11.

HTHA. Huntington Town Historian's Archives, Huntington, NY.

Lincoln, Charles Z. 1894. *The Colonial Laws of New York from 1664 to the Revolution.* Albany: New York State.

MID. Montauk Indian Deeds, Brooklyn Historical Society Archives, Collections no. 1974, location VI, 0, folders 1–6, Brooklyn, NY.

NYCD. 1856–87. *Documents Relative to the Colonial History of the State of New York,* ed. Edmund Bailey O'Callaghan and Berthold Fernow. 15 vols. Albany: Weed Parsons and Sons.

RCNP. 1859. *Records of the Colony of New Plymouth,* ed. David Pulsifer. Boston: William White. (Vol. 9 and 10 include the Acts of the Commissioners of the United Colonies, 1643–1679.)

RTBH. 1932. *Records of the Town of Brookhaven, Book B, 1679–1756.* New York: The Derrydale Press.

RTEH. 1877–1905. *Records of the Town of East Hampton.* 5 vols. Sag Harbor, NY: John Hunt.

RTH. 1887–1889. *Records of the Town of Huntington,* ed. Charles Street. 3 vols. Huntington: Town of Huntington.

RTNSH. 1896–1904. *Records of the Towns of North and South Hempstead,* ed. Benjamin Hicks. 8 vols. Jamaica: Long Island Farmer Print.

RTS. 1882. *Records of the Town of Southold,* ed. J. Wickham Case. 3 vols. Southold: Towns of Riverhead and Southold.

RTSH. 1874–1928. *Records of the Town of Southampton,* ed. William Pelletreau. 8 vols. Sag Harbor: John Hunt.

SHTA. Southampton Town Archives, Town Clerk's Office, Southampton, NY.

Wooley, Charles. 1968. "Two Years' Journal in New York, 1678–80." In *Historical Chronicles of New Amsterdam, Colonial New York and Early Long Island,* ed. Cornell Jaray. Port Washington, NY: Ira J. Friedman.

Secondary Sources

Adams, James Truslow. 1918. *A History of the Town of Southampton.* Reprint; Port Washington: Ira J. Friedman, 1962.

Edwards, Everett, and Jeanette Rattray. 1932. *Whale-off: The Story of American Shore Whaling.* Reprint; New York: Coward and McCann, 1956.

Galenson, David W. 1981. *White Servitude in Colonial America: An Economic Analysis.* London: Cambridge University Press.

Hawke, David Freeman. 1988. *Everyday Life in Early America.* New York: Harper and Row.

Helms, Mary. 1969. "The Purchase Society: Adaptation to Economic Frontiers." *Anthropological Quarterly,* 21 (4): 325–42.

———. 1971. *Asang: Adaptations to Culture Contact in a Miskito Community,* Gainesville: University of Florida Press.

Jernegan, Marcus Wilson. 1931. *Laboring and Dependent Classes in Colonial America.* New York: Frederick Ungar.

Kross, Jessica. 1983. *The Evolution of an American Town: Newtown, New York, 1642–1775.* Philadelphia: Temple University Press.

Leacock, Eleanor. 1954. "The Montagnais Hunting Territory and the Fur Trade." *Anthropological Association Memoir,* no. 78.

Lauber, Almon Wheeler. 1913. *Indian Slavery in Colonial Times Within the Present Limits of the United States.* New York: Columbia University Press.

Linton, Ralph, ed. 1963. *Acculturation in Seven American Indian Tribes.* New York: P. Smith.

Lott, Roy. 1964. "Indentured Servants in Huntington." *Long Island Forum* 22 (6): 125–6.

Marshall, Bernice Schultz. 1962 *Colonial Hempstead: Long Island Life Under the Dutch and English.* Port Washington: I. J. Friedman. This was originally published in 1937 under the name Bernice Schultz.

McKee, Samuel. 1935. *Labor in Colonial New York, 1664–1776.* Reprint; Port Washington: Ira J. Friedman, 1965.

Moss, Richard Shannon. 1993. *Slavery on Long Island: A Study in Local Institutional and Early American Life.* New York: Garland Publishing.

Murphey, Robert F. 1964. "Social Change and Acculturation." *Transactions of the New York Academy of Science.* Series 2, 26 (7): 845–54.

Ostrander, Stephen M. *A Hisory of the City of Brooklyn and Kings County.* Brooklyn.

Papageorge, Toby. 1983. "Records of the Shinnecock Trustees." In *The Shinnecock Indians: A Culture History,* ed. Gaynell Stone, 141–225. Stony Brook: Suffolk County Archaeological Association (hereafter SCAA).

Scott, Kenneth. 1961. "The New York Slave Insurrection of 1712." *New York Historical Society Quarterly* 45: 43–74.

Seybolt, Robert Francis. 1917. *Apprenticeship and Apprenticeship Education in Colonial New England and New York.* New York: Columbia University Press.

Spicer, Edward. 1962. *Perspectives in American Indian Culture Change.* Chicago: University of Chicago Press.

Strong John A. 1983. "How The Land Was Lost." In *The Shinnecock Indians: A Culture History,* ed. Gaynell Stone, 53–117. Stony Brook, NY: SCAA.

——. 1989. "Shinnecock and Montauk Whalemen." *The Long Island Historical Journal* 2 (1): 29–40.

——. 1990. "The Pigskin Book: Records of Native American Whalemen." *The Long Island Historical Journal* 3 (1): 17–29.

——. 1991. "The Long Frontier: Fiction and Folklore." *The Long Island Historical Journal,* 3(2): 253–8.

——. 1993. "The Thirteen Tribes of Long Island: The History of a Myth." *Hudson Valley Regional Review* 9 (2): 39–73.

——. 1994. "The Imposition of Colonial Jurisdiction over the Montauk Indians of Long Island." *Ethnohistory* 44 (Fall 1994): 561–90.

Strong, Lara M. and Selcuk Karabag. 1991. "Quashawam: Sunksquaw of the Montauk." *Long Island Historical Journal* 3 (2): 189–204.

Vickers, Daniel. 1983. "The First Whalemen of Nantucket," *William and Mary Quarterly* 40: 560–83.

White, Richard. 1983. *The Roots of Dependency.* Lincoln: University of Nebraska Press.

——. 1991. *The Middle Ground.* New York: Cambridge Univ. Press.

The c. 1795 Kissam House at 434 Park Avenue was the site of "A Child's Work and Play" education program by the Huntington Historical Society.

"A Child's Work and Play": Hands-on Learning in a Historic House and Barn

Laura MacDermeid

With an Epilogue by Rosemary Sloggatt

For over ninety years the Huntington Historical Society has taught Long Islanders about the material culture and social history of central Long Island. Historical collections and programs have special importance in a suburban region such as ours, with its highly mobile and largely non-native population. The Society reaches out with its broad and varied programs to an equally varied constituency, and is important for providing a sense of place in a rapidly changing environment

The Society owns and operates two museum houses—the David Conklin Farmhouse (c. 1750) furnished to reflect the stages of its construction (Colonial, Federal, and Victorian) and the Kissam House (c. 1795), home to two generations of Huntington physicians and reinterpreted and restored in the early 1980s. (Earlier the society had designated the latter as the Powell-Jarvis House.) In addition, the Society owns the Huntington Sewing and Trade School (c. 1905) where its research library and offices are located.

In 1982, the Huntington Historical Society created a separate Education Department staffed by a full-time Education Curator and a part-time Museum Teacher. This was the first step in the Society's long-range goal of updating and expanding programs both for the public and for schools. Prompted by the New York State Board of Regents mandate that fourth grade students study local history, the Department's first Curator, Leslie Roth, and Museum Teacher, Dorothy Stone, developed a hands-on workshop. The workshop was specifically designed to provide assistance to fourth grade teachers, who were hard pressed to find resources within their communities to help them teach local history.

Objectives

Out of many hours of research and collaboration with educators came "A Child's Work and Play: 1800–1840." The goals of this program were many: utilize a marvelous facility, the Kissam House Barn, to its best potential; increase the audience of the Huntington Historical Society by using the enthusiasm of children to reach adults; teach about the material culture of Long Island and of the Town of Huntington by discussing and examining actual objects used by Long Island residents more than 150 years ago; address the daily activities of everyday families; discuss what a fourth grader might have done on a typical day in the early 1800s; provide an opportunity for students to work at chores and play games which the fourteen Kissam children might have experienced; increase the number of days when facilities were available for field trip bookings.

Method: Pre-visit

The workshop development was a collaborative effort between Society staff and area educators. A panel of educators was formed to advise on development and consisted of teachers, principals, and curriculum development people from seven of the eight school districts in the Town of Huntington.

It was decided that a pre-visit packet was in order, so that teachers and students could be well prepared for their museum visit. The packet is sent to the teacher two weeks in advance of the visit along with a set of slides. Teachers receive guidelines for their visit, a map of our properties, a slide script, puzzles, poems, recipes, and suggested activities for before or after the museum visit. Among the poems is "The Farmer" by Zophar Ketcham, Huntington resident, found in an 1833 copybook belonging to fourteen year old Conklin Baylis. (A copy of the poem is found on page 53–5.) The poem describes the seasons of the Long Island farmer and harkens back to the day when daily activities were dictated by harvests and livestock. For some students, and even some teachers, this is their first realization that Long Island was not always a suburb. This kind of pre-visit preparation means that children come to the program prepared for what will take place. They have already seen the house exterior and some of the rooms. They are able to identify easily with many of the objects and tasks. Time spent at the museum is thus used efficiently, and students and teachers alike arrive at the Kissam House filled with anticipation and excitement.

The Tour

"A Child's Work and Play" is a three-hour program. The Museum Teacher along with a volunteer school docent arrive early to set up the house and barn. The arriving class is greeted at the front door where the Museum Teacher discusses museum rules with the students and adults (a must in an institution where 95 percent of displayed objects are not behind glass or roped off in any way). The group splits in two, and half begin upstairs with one guide and the other half downstairs with the other. Teachers are asked to have their students wear name tags. This not only facilitates easy management within the museum (a child reaching for a fragile object who is called by name is stopped in his tracks!), but it also provides for a very personal tour for both parties.

The tour begins in the front hall where the guide discusses the Kissam family, how they came to Huntington from Glen Cove, why they chose to live on the Village Green or Town Spotte, the place of the Town Spotte in the lives of early Long Islanders, and why this area is less and less the center of Town activity. The guide sets the stage for the children by emphasizing the role of the children in this family. She may discuss the floorboards and stair treads as she describes the work of the carpenter Timothy Jarvis, who built the house for Dr. Kissam. She might discuss the leather fire bucket and linen pillow case hanging in the hall, their use in an early Long Island community, and their replacements today.

Next, the guide leads the children into the back parlor or "eating parlor." There she might briefly discuss the work of Dr. Kissam by showing the various medical instruments and books and the bill for medical services performed, all of which are located in the back parlor cupboard. Various items are usually set out on the mantle, some of which can be passed around for the children to examine themselves. Items such as homemade soap, a candlemold, sugar nippers, a pierced lantern, a flint and steel, and a mortar and pestle are discussed. The guide emphasizes the role of the child in using these items. She also emphasizes the basics of everyday life in this house during the time period—heating, lighting, food preparation, transportation. She might give the children a chance to examine, with a partner, one of the pieces of cast iron cooking equipment: a waffle iron, toaster, tea pot, or cauldron. She discusses the types of furniture found in the room and how it can easily be folded up and pushed against the walls to make space for this large family. She might point out the type of rug on the floor and ask how it was made and who might have made it. The George Washington lithograph over the fireplace provides an opportunity to talk about the 1790 tour of Long Island and the stop which the President made up the street at the Widow Platt's Tavern, where the food was "tolerably good." All of this "discussion" does not take place in the form of a lecture but rather as sort of a mutual discovery, with plenty of questions asked of the children and time allowed for them to figure out answers for themselves. Each guide endeavors always to make a connection between past and present and between the fourteen Kissam children and the children in her group.

Next, the children pass through the "north bed chamber," noting its simple furniture and linsey-woolsey coverlet. The coverlet provides an opportunity to discuss early Long Island textiles and how they differed from those we use today. The group then moves through the passage into the front parlor. In the front parlor they examine the much more decorative furnishings, floorcloth, and window hangings and are asked to consider what kinds of activities happened in this parlor as compared to the back parlor. Often a little time is spent in the front parlor talking about the research done in order to make the change from the Powell-Jarvis House (as it was formerly known) to the Kissam House and why this was done. I like to discuss the things which were found beneath the floorboards (a piece of floorcloth and a little toy wooden boat among others) and to describe the infra-red cameras used by the architectural historians who studied the frame of the house (they looked like Ghostbusters!). An attempt is made to help the children understand that we are still studying the people who lived here and the kinds of lives they had in order to understand what we are doing on Long Island today.

The group next travels up the stairs to the bed chamber (the second group in the meantime has come down and headed for the back parlor). In the bedchamber they discuss the canopy bed and its hangings. They pull out the trundle beneath, look at the ropes holding the mattress, perhaps try out the bed key to tighten the ropes. Again, they see the efficient use of space and resources by this early family. The chamber chair and washstand might lead to a discussion of stencilling (something they have a chance to try later in the barn) and the lack of plumbing in the house. The guide might try the "interview an artifact" technique with the footstove or the bed warmer. (This is a questioning strategy which leads to detailed examination and analysis of an artifact.) The footstool and bedwarmer also lend themselves to a discussion about early area craftsmen and their roles within the community. The panelling in the bed chamber gives the guide another chance to talk about the carpenter Timothy Jarvis and how his talents helped to make this a special house, a town house, for the Kissams. Students are informed that later in the barn they will have a chance to use woodworking tools similar to those Mr. Jarvis might have used to make this house. The guide might also discuss the bandboxes in the room and their use for storage, the quill pen (another item which will be used later), and the chairs near the fire.

The last room the group visits before heading to the barn is the child's chamber. This room, with its tea set and toy desk, allows a chance to again discuss those fourteen Kissam children. The two early maps on the wall, drawn by Abby Seaman as a student at the Huntington Academy in the 1840s, provide an opportunity to talk about early schooling in Huntington and the Kissam family's role in the Huntington Academy. The guide then leads her group back down the stairs and out to the barn. If the other group is not awaiting them, the class might stop at the stock and pillory in the yard to try them out and discuss their use in an early Long Island community.

"Hands-on"

The barn is where the hands-on portion of the program takes place. First, the Museum Teacher introduces the barn, talks about its relocation to the Kissam House property, talks about the role of Dr. Kissam as farmer/physician, and discusses the use of the barn and outbuildings of a typical Long Island farming family during this time. Next, the Museum Teacher walks the class through each of the five hands-on stations. Trial and error method was used in developing these stations. During sessions with pilot classes, many activities were tried—herb garden tending, drying apples, making corn husk dolls, making brooms, dipping candles. The five hands-on stations which emerged as most popular and easiest to administer on a daily basis during the program were: woodworking, flax preparation, stencilling and writing with quill pens, weaving on a tape loom, and spinning wool on a drop spindle. The whole class participates in butter churning.

All five of the activity stations involve crafts and tasks from the 1800–1840 period. All were common on Long Island. The class divides into five groups and has about ten minutes at each station. At the woodworking station they work with a bucksaw, a plane, and a drill and bit. They also use wooden pegs and penny nails. Time spent at this station involves examining the mortise and tenon construction of the sheep shed where the tools are set up. Next the children move to the flax station where they are able to process the plant from the point where it has been harvested to where it is able to be put on a wheel and spun. While demonstrating the art of braking, scutching, and hackling flax, the Museum Teacher also discusses the use of flax by families such as the Kissams, its prolific growth on Long Island during this period, and how common its end product—linen—was in the homes of early Huntington families. The Museum Teacher makes a connection between the textiles seen in the house—linen sheets, linsey-woolsey coverlets, clothing—and the process employed in this station. Stencilling and quill pens are the next station and here the how and why of these two forms of decoration and communication are discussed. Copper stencils which served to produce signs on cider barrels are passed around, and this can lead to a discussion about the Newtown Pippin, Long Island's own apple, and its use in the 1800s home. Weaving on a tape loom is the fourth station. Instruction here takes some doing because it is a task which is generally foreign to most twentieth century Long Islanders. It was, however, an everyday activity for children the age of this class during the early 1800s. Weaving on a tape loom produced belts, straps, and many other useful items for an early family. The last station is spinning, and here the children learn about how wool proceeds from the back of the sheep to the wool blanket. When they reach this station, they have a chance to tease, card, and spin their own piece of yarn and to examine the sheep shears and niddy noddy, two items which assisted in the process. The Museum Teacher explains the many uses of this animal and how common a sight it was on early Long Island. Nothing is more hands-on for the students than the greasy lanolin which the raw wool leaves on their hands!

Adult participation is crucial to the success of "A Child's Work and Play." Each adult is assigned a station to supervise. The teacher is asked to stay with the woodworking (for obvious reasons of safety), the docent and Museum Teacher assist with spinning and weaving, and parent chaperones are asked to stay at the flax and stencilling areas. Not only does this make accompanying parents feel like part of the action, it helps them to learn something new also. Their response has been overwhelmingly positive throughout the course of this workshop.

After the class has moved through the five stations, they reassemble in the second bay of the barn. Lunches are handed out, and the butter churning begins. Each student and adult has a chance to come up and churn while eating lunch. The whole process and use of butter is discussed. Corn bread or "johnnycake," which has been warming in the Kissam kitchen oven, is brought out, and everyone gets to taste the results of their churning.

After lunch the class has a chance to play a period game—usually Buzz because Blind Man's Bluff has proved a little too active at this point in the day. Students get a chance to practice multiplication tables, just as early Kissam children did while playing this game. If the children should miss their turn, they must part with a shoe. In order to get their shoe back, they must pay a "forfeit"—answer a question about their tour, perform a tongue twister, answer a riddle. The visit always ends on a happy note when, with shoes intact, the group boards the bus and heads back to school.

Follow Up

While developing this program, Society staff members and advisors realized the importance of sending students home with something that lets them remember their visit. Not only do they take with them the flax, the spun yarn, and the stencil, but also a flyer with puzzles and games that relate to what they have learned. Included in the flyer is a note to parents which reiterates the facilities and hours of the Huntington Historical Society and invites them to return for another visit. Each teacher also receives flyers on any upcoming Society programs for posting in the classroom. Time and time again, we see children who have come with their classes return to our museum houses with their families in tow. They are usually able to remember, demonstrate, and even involve other visitors in what they learned during their workshop.

The time invested in research and development of this program has been repaid many times. Docents who teach the workshop primarily receive "on the job" training, supported by relevant reading material. Motivating docents and staff is no problem at all because the rewards are so great. The teachers who were instrumental in the program's development returned each year with a new classe. They also participate in other Society programs such as in-service seminars. One retired teacher even joined the docent corps. At the Huntington Historical Society, we believe that "A Child's Work and Play" is an example of local history at its finest.

Epilogue

Rosemary Sloggatt

In the years since its creation, the program "A Child's Work and Play" has had a far-reaching impact on the Society's education programs. The Society has long been convinced of the importance of "knowing the place." The Society's constitution states its purpose to be preserving the history of the Town of Huntington and stimulating interest in preserving sites of historical value. How that mission is achieved, of course, has changed through the years.

We first began offering school programs in 1923, twenty years after the Society's founding. A child visiting the Conklin House, then the Society's headquarters, would have viewed several rooms of the house which held flat cases containing items of importance to Huntington's past.

In 1953, in conjunction with the Town's Tricentennial, the Conklin House exhibits were reinterpreted. Period room settings were created to help the visitor understand the house in its historic context, and the Society's first formal education program, "A Visit to Old Huntington," was created. This program was designed to be administered by tour guides who would offer the specifics of Huntington's history for the period indicated by the room settings.

In the early 1980s the restoration of the Kissam house and the addition of a period barn invited new possibilities for interpretation. Unlike the Conklin house, this exhibit offered not a series of period rooms grouped to convey the passage of time, but instead showed an entire house of one period, as it were, frozen in time. This type of exhibition translated readily into "a day in the life" programming.

"A Child's Work and Play," the program created out of that interpretation, reflects not only ideas presented by the restoration but many new educational methods including whole learning, contextual interpretation (viewing the exhibit from the child's point of view) and, most significantly, experiential, or hands-on learning. In response to New York State's Regents Action Plan, school districts searching for ways to teach social history within their local community found a resource in the Society's new program.

The Society offered "A Child's Work and Play" for ten years. Although the Society no longer offers this program, many of its best aspects have been incorporated into other programs.

One of the program's greatest strengths was its relaxed pace and its high adult-to-child ratio. As school districts found budgets squeezed, they began looking for programs that could accommodate a full bus load, or two classes of children. The Society was forced to offer simultaneous programs at the Kissam and Conklin houses in order to accommodate such large numbers. A second slide set was created for the Conklin house to offer a similar pre-visit experience. These cutbacks, a shrinking volunteer pool, and the loss of the museum teacher position in 1985 made offering the program on a daily basis increasingly difficult.

In 1990, the Society began offering a one-week summer program for area children based on "A Child's Work and Play" which is entitled "Passport to the Past." Enrollment was limited to twenty children per session and the activities were expanded to include cooking and other pertinent crafts and trades from the period, including basketweaving and blacksmithing. The value of this experience is attested to by the fact that the program has grown each year. It is now offered as four two-week sessions throughout the summer.

The approach of the Society's one hundredth anniversary (2003), the proliferation of similar cultural institutions, and recent economic and demographic changes on Long Island have caused the institution to reexamine its role in the community. In response to these and other factors, a five-year museum education plan, funded by New York State Council on the Arts, was completed in 1993. This important planning document forms the basis for insuring that the Society's educational programming continues to provide a sense of place into the twenty-first century.

* * *

On the following pages are examples of some of the materials orginally developed by Leslie Roth in the pre-visit packet for "A Child's Work and Play." (Editor.)

Pre-Visit Packet Contents

[*   indicates items included below]
*   Cover letter to teacher
1. Slide program and script for Kissam House.
*2. Mystery Message Puzzle
3. Matching Puzzle
*4. Suggested Pre and Post-Visit activities
5. Directions for 19th Century Games and Recipe for Corn Bread
6. Directions for making Corn Husk Dolls
7. Seasonal excerpts from *The New England Farmer*, 1822
*8. "The Farmer," a poem by Zophar Ketcham (1746–1837), resident of Huntington, copied by Conklin Baylis in 1833 at the age of 14.
*9. Suggested activities for use with "The Farmer."

The Huntington Historical Society
209 Main Street, Huntington, New York 11743
(516) 427–7045

Important****Important****Important****Important

Dear Teacher:

We are looking forward to your visit to the "Child's Work and Play" hands-on workshop on _____ from_____ to_____.

The workshop program offers the students the opportunity to see and experience the objects, furnishings, tools, and crafts which were familiar to an early 19th century family. Your class will be met by a Museum Teacher and a Museum Volunteer who will guide them through the Kissam House and the activities in the Barn.

Enclosed is a pre-visit packet designed to help prepare you for your visit to the Kissam House. Rental of the accompanying slide set is included in the price of admission. The booklet is yours to keep. *The slides MUST be returned on the day of your visit* (where multiple classes are visiting from the same school, one set of slides is enclosed, to be returned by the last teacher). A fee of $5 per day will be charged if these slides are not returned on the day of your visit.

May we remind you:

- Payment is due *two weeks* before your visit and is *non-refundable*. Make checks payable to the Huntington Historical Society and mail to: Huntington Historical Society, 209 Main Street, Huntington, NY 11743, Attn: Education Department. The fee is $3 per student with a minimum of $50 per class.
- At least three adults (including teacher) MUST accompany each class. There is no charge for adults. *Adults are expected to participate and to stay with the class.*
- Class size is limited to 30 students. You will be charged for an additional class if you arrive with more than the limit.
- Students and adults should wear name tags (see sample).
- Students should not wear their "best clothes" as this is a "hands-on" workshop.
- Students and adults should bring lunch and a drink. During *spring season only,* buttered cornbread will be served as part of the workshop.
- The workshop runs 2-1/2 hours in fall, 3 hours in spring. Please plan accordingly. We must forego some activities in the event of a late arrival.
- A souvenir cart is available with inexpensive items (25 cents-$2) which relate to our programs. Please plan an additional 10 minutes or more if your students wish to purchase.

The Huntington Historical Society prides itself on its strong commitment to education in the areas of local and regional history. We offer many additional programs and services. Please contact us for further information.

Mystery Message Puzzle

Directions: Write the correct answer in the blank spaces and circle the letter or letters in spaces with an asterisk and you will uncover a secret message.

1. Six square miles deeded to Huntington's original settlers was called the _ _ _   _ _ _ _ _ _ _ * *
2. The fabric made from flax is called _ _ _ * _
3. Two water buckets could be carried on a * * _ _
4. Boys and girls made feather pens which were called _ * _ _ _ _
5. Many things were traded in old Huntington. Another word for trade is _ * _ * _ _
6. A craftsman who worked with iron was called a _ _ _ _ _ _ _ _ _ _ * *
7. The man who ground your grain into flour was called a _ _ _ _ _ *
8. Girls would use this to weave belts _ _ * _   _ * _ _
9. Sheep would be raised so that the family would have * _ _ _
10. In order to remove all the tow, the flax was drawn through a * _ _ _ _ _ *
11. A family's main source of light was _ _ _ _ _ * _ _
12. In 1800, boys and girls had many chores or * _ _ _
13. The plant which was made into fiber is called _ _ * _
14. The most important grain raised by Long Island farmers was _ _ * _
15. After you spin the flax or wool, you would take the thread to a _ _ _ * _
16. The Sammis mill, used to saw wood, was powered by _ _ * _ _
17. Children worked hard, played and also went to * _ * _ * _
18. To save space, smaller children would sleep in a _ _ * _ _ _   _ _ _
19. Girls would learn how to do many things when they made their * _ _ _   _ * _

Answers: school, candles, jobs, quills, trundle bed, wool, old purchase, tape loom, wind, flax, yoke, blacksmith, sampler, weaver, barter, miller, hetchel, linen, corn

Suggested Activities to Use and Do
Before or After Your Visit to the Museum

1. Discuss what a historic house museum is and the rules that should be followed during your visit. (Grades 1-7)

2. Have the children interview parents and grandparents (orally or by letter) about what life was like when they were young: chores, transportation, leisure activities, television, food

preparation, men and women's roles, etc. How have things changed? Have they gotten easier? better? of just different? Why have things changed? (Grades 3-7)

3. Discuss with children (grades 1-3 perhaps) or have older children find out the "how" and "where it comes from" then and now of: (a) candles; (b) cider; (c) spices; (d) soap; (e) tea; (f) butter; (g) fabric; (h) leather; (i) flour. Who made these common household things in 1800? Who or what makes them now? How has the production process changed?

4. Have the children discuss or investigate different craftsmen of the 19th century: tanner, dyer, weaver, hatmaker, carpenter, pewterer, shipwright, printer, cooper, housewright, gunsmith, wheelwright, blacksmith, chandler, etc. (Grades 1-7)

5. Bake a batch or two of gingerbread and/or make cornhusk dolls. (Grades 1-7)

6. Play some "old" games that are still being played today such as "Blind Man's Buff" or "Buzz" (great for multiplication skills) or "Hide and Seek" or "Tag."

7. Have the children discuss the song, "Pop! Goes The Weasel." Do they know the words and what they mean? Try to find a weasel in the Kissam House.

"Pop! Goes The Weasel"

All around the cobbler's bench,
The monkey chased the weasel.
The monkey thought 'twas all in fun,
Pop! goes the weasel.

A penny for a spool of thread,
A penny for a needle
That's the way the money goes,
Pop! goes the weasel!

Yarn reel. Arrow shows weasel which clicked after a certain amount of wool had been wound.

"The Farmer"
by Zophar Ketcham
As copied by Conklin Baylis, 14 years old, in 1833.

Some exhortation
To farmers of every station
Farmer from far and farmers near

Of what I relate you may all hear
When the harvest is ripe then we should begin
Then we should be careful and gather it clean
Let us be sure we never do sleep
When we should be cradling or when we should reap
For fear of shame and confusion of face
Our grain would be wasted with shame and disgrace
Then let us be prudent and gather it clean
Then turn in our hogs the stubble to glean
Then comes our oats as well as our flax
To feed up our horses and cover our backs.
So let us all act with prudence and care
Then we all the better shall fare.
When the oats and the flax are all stored away
Then to the meadows and marsh for our hay
Observe the tide look at the wind
See well to your work that it comes not behind
Look out for a breeze and take the first gale
For fear of the oar instead of the sail
Lay up a good store for winter to come
So if it be tedious we all may have some
Hay time is past cold weather comes on
Come boys now we will gather our corn
Let us then gather as soon as will do
If we have no old we must have new
When the corn is all gathered and safe in the crib
Then see that our hogs are thick on the rib
So we shall have bread and we shall have meat
And all that is good then for us to eat.
Cows give us milk sheep find us wool
Our backs to be warm and our bellies be full
Now let us lay up a good pile of wood
That in cold weather you'll find it is good
When winter is come and the snow get deep
Take care of your cows as well as your sheep
Thresh out your grain dress out your flax
Tis food for our bellies and clothes for our back,
Feed up your Horses to ride in the slay
And so the winter will soon wear a way
When winter is gone and the spring comes now
Let every Farmer be jogging his plough

Plough up his land with prudence and care
And puts in his seed for a nethermore year
Put in his corn in the month of May
In the month of June begin on his hay
To be careful and prudent then let us all try
Twill bring a good harvest I hope in July
In August then cultivate well your ground
And that will bring the year just round
Be careful then and sow good seed
Twil bring a new harvest in time of need
So let us act with prudance and care
Then we all the better shall fare
You put it under your shelf
He that is wise is wise for himself
But he that exhortation doth scorn
Will come out the little end of the horn.

Suggested Activities to Use with "The Farmer"

1. Listening and listing: Have the children list activities and chores performed in each season. Then read the poem aloud and have them add to their seasonal lists. Can they think of other chores that might not be listed such as preserving food, etc.? Don't forget the chores and jobs done by the women and children. Have the children draw contrasts and comparisons between the list and what they are familiar with now.

2. Write a letter to a friend in a nearby town (Oyster Bay, for example) as if it were 1800. Talk about school, daily activities, the weather, the farm animals, the chores, etc.

3. A Child's Diary: Have the children read the poem in class, aloud or to themselves. Discuss the difficult and different words and concepts with them. What can they learn about daily life from these selections? Have each child write a diary for one week in each season as if they were the age they are now, but in the year 1800. (A good resource for this is Eric Sloane, *Diary of An American Boy*.) Stress the seasonal aspect of life and the constant preoccupation with weather which *all* diaries of the time stresses. Why? Farmers are absolutely dependent on the weather and heat was a constant concern and problem.

The Creation of a Students' Local History Journal: Amityville, New York in the Twentieth Century

Charles F. Howlett

What can students themselves do to make history come alive? Publish a local history journal is my response. For me, the role of a history teacher should be to conduct a course based on historical inquiry, theory, and visual contact with primary documents. Such a course is feasible with Advanced Placement history students in high school and very capable students on the junior high and elementary level. In the lower grades the journal can be scaled down to suit their intellectual curiosity and maturation. In my case, as a high school teacher, the journal was aimed at a more sophisticated level. Naturally, I have always been excited by the possibility of what Jacques Barzun, the noted Columbia University historian and administrator, fittingly coined "two minds sharing one thought."[1]

Of course, this goal is an ideal, but it is one well worth trying to reach. I became motivated by the challenging possibility of many minds sharing in the single process of historical creativity. I wanted students to remove themselves from an emphasis on a fact-oriented approach, commonly found in high schools which teach students to pass a state or Regents' test, to one encouraging them to recreate the local past through the use of their own inquiring minds. In other words, I wanted them to dig deeper into problem-solving— asking the "hows" and "whys" of events, personalities and actions.

Objective

My purpose in creating a student history journal was to encourage students "to understand clearly that history puts its emphasis on 'the facts' not for their own sake but for the sake of the meanings they can actually be seen to carry."[2] In particular, I wanted to impress upon them that sound historical scholarship proceeds best with materials that are original sources. For students to reach more sophisticated levels of historical inquiry, a teacher must develop assignments, based on primary sources, that call attention to areas of controversy and are subject to differing interpretation, each calling into play standards of good historical work. It is not enough for them merely to accept what is found in print, but to examine as well the way in which historians arrive at their conclusions. It was my hope that if students were asked to research and write a creative paper using original sources, they would not only be testing their own ability to make sound historical judgments but also understanding how historians work at deriving answers to questions.

In seeking to make history come alive in the students' eyes, I encouraged them during the first week of class to consider the prospect of working mainly with local primary sources (e. g., diaries, autobiographies, interviews, personal letters, village board minutes, oral history memoirs, newspapers, census data) to understand more clearly how Amityville residents lived and reacted to particular events and situations during their lifetimes. I wanted my students to gain firsthand experience with original materials, and I wanted them to work with those materials in order to record their own perception of the past. If history is a record of the past, I informed them, then the record—the original sources—must be allowed to speak for itself through the pens of those examining it.

I also wanted to impress upon them that using local history sources would lend itself to a clearer understanding of the meaning and importance of historical change. If teachers are interested in having their students learn to think critically and carefully, to develop a feeling for their community and their nation, to understand the world about them in terms of cause and effect, to develop ideals of integrity and responsibility, I argued, then using the data of local history will help them reach these objectives. How a community changes over time adds a new dimension of depth to critical thinking: a weighing of cause and result, an understanding of public opinion, prejudice, personal likes and dislikes, and the healing effects of time. As Ralph Adams Brown and William G. Tyrrell remind us: "The ability to reason soundly, judge wisely, and draw independent and temperate conclusions are essential qualities for all citizens. Local history affords numerous possibilities for acquiring these skills."[3]

Preparation

As a means of tackling this project I recommended they read chapters one, two, four, six, and eleven through sixteen of Jacques Barzun and Henry F. Graff's *The Modern Researcher* (New York: Harcourt, Brace, Jovanovich, 1985) as well as William Strunk and E. B. White's *The Elements of Style* (New York: Macmillan, 1959). Both books were purchased by the school district, and copies were made available to each student. I wanted to instill two fundamental ideas in their minds: first, sound historical scholarship requires careful analysis and reflection; second, interesting history demands good writing based on hard editing and revision. Consequently, during the first month of class I set aside three class periods to discuss the assigned readings from both books. The mechanics of writing a research paper were clearly delineated by Barzun and Graff. Students found this book extremely helpful in terms of defining a topic, taking notes, organizing a paper, and utilizing "practical imagination at work." At the same time, they were equally appreciative of Strunk and White's method of pointing out the rules of usage and principles of composition most commonly violated. During one class discussion, for example, a student commented that she thought I was a social studies teacher, not an English teacher. I politely responded by reminding all the students that history is also literature, and for history to be read, appreciated, and understood it must be written well. Throughout the course of their research I instructed them to use both books as constant reference tools and, most importantly, when writing their papers always to keep their audience in mind—because ultimately their audience would judge their contribution.

To impress upon them further the seriousness of this project, I invited a guest speaker to address the class on historical research and writing. In this case the speaker, Barbara Kelly, now Curator of the Long Island Studies Institute and Special Collections at Hofstra University, talked about her Master's thesis on the changing architectural designs of homes in late nineteenth and early twentieth-century Amityville. Armed with photos, census data, family records, personal accounts by former local village leaders, and newspapers, this budding social historian demonstrated how over a period of time architectural designs were affected by the social and economic changes taking place within the community. During her enlightening presentation,

Ms. Kelly emphasized the need for writing original papers that were not simply a summarization of ideas gleaned from secondary works (an altogether common habit among high school—and even college—students). If our journal was to be an original contribution to historical scholarship, she added, it was necessary to work with primary sources. "What neat discoveries can you come up with after examining the materials?" she asked. With all her research materials in front of her, including two boxes of note cards, this proved to be an invaluable lesson in the search for new evidence. The students were impressed by the historian at work with the tools of the trade, and by her attempt to recreate the past in written form through careful examination of primary sources.

It was extremely important to emphasize the point that this local research project was more than just a traditional term paper. Yet how were these students to make the leap from high school to college level writing based on original sources and insight? My answer was to generate interest in the publication of a high school history journal—something a cut above the average term paper in terms of scholarly research and writing. The incentive, of course, was to emphasize the importance of writing for publication. One must realize, to state the obvious to teachers as well as students, that even very bright students do not possess the maturity and sophistication of scholars whose publications reflect years of research and analysis. Thus, I pointed out that their projects would be more easy to write if they wrote "history close to home"—that is if they focused on local individuals and organizations. This point was crucial to the success of the journal as well as to the task of helping students select, narrow, and organize their topics. Clarity of presentation in print was the overriding goal.

Methodology

Organizationally, the assignment was presented during the first week of class. A timetable was established in which a comprehensive outline had to be submitted during the first week of January, a rough draft turned in the first week of March, and the finished product completed a month later. Therefore, after topics were selected and appropriate sources located, students visited, on their own, the richly endowed historical society, the village library, notable families in the village as well as in North

Amityville, long-established businesses, school officials, village trustees, police and fire department officials and church leaders. I first made sure enough information was available from the local historical society. This was duly accomplished at the start of the school year when the village historian, Mr. Seth Purdy, assured me that ample documentation existed from the turn of the century to the present. I also made sure that the students developed an appropriate set of questions to ask when interviewing local residents and officials. Thus, the skills of oral history gathering were also practiced in recreating their community's past. Finally, the students themselves placed a notice about the project in the *Amityville Record* in order to obtain more information on their projects.

The results were impressive. What I found most rewarding was the students' ability to interview residents with precision and insight. They had done their homework well: it was clear that they had read thoroughly all available sources related to their topic. In producing a local history journal it was necessary to confine our research to the first half of the twentieth century. This was designed on purpose because documents were more abundant as was the availability of older residents still living in the community. Students expressed a sense of appreciation and satisfaction in not only learning how to write history but also what kind of community they were living in.

Through the use of newspaper accounts, business records, school reports, church accounts, personal interviews, library and local history sources, and public documents, students acquired a greater understanding of how Amityville developed as a community from the turn of the century to the Second World War. One paper, for instance, discussed how village families survived during the Great Depression; we learned that "persistence" and "determination" were key factors. Another paper told the story of how Black families in North Amityville (Sunrise Highway acts as the northern boundary line for the village of Amityville) handled the depression: "The people dug in and worked hard to survive, and . . . they did." Their suffering, it was learned, was not unlike that of their white counterparts who lived in the village to the south.

The growth of churches was found to have been the result of a growing population, which in turn reflected the expansion of the railroad and the new highway construction. Similarly, the police and fire departments had expanded to meet the needs of a growing population. Racial concerns were part of the school system's life then as they are today. We found out that in 1925 the Ku Klux Klan selected the topic "Our Flag" for a grammar school essay. In the late 1930s, a group of Black parents came before the Board of Education to protest alleged verbal abuse and academic discrimination. And finally, politics was "as usual." In the 1935 mayoral election, one of the journal articles noted, both political parties, the Union Party and the People's Party, called for lower taxes. Some things never change.

Production

Since this was intended to be a student history journal, a student editorial committee was chosen to select the best papers for publication. The committee was selected on the basis of my prior analysis of six critical book reviews completed during the course and consultation with the students' English teachers. Once the committee was established, I set aside three days after school to discuss chapter sixteen of *The Modern Researcher* in conjunction with *Historian's Handbook* by Wood Gray, et al.[4] Barzun and Graff's "Revising for Printer and Public" is rewarding in its clear presentation of a step by step approach to editing works for publication. (I photocopied the back cover of *Historian's Handbook*, containing the symbols used for proofreading, and distributed copies to those students who were asked to revise and retype their articles for the journal.) Then, along with the instructor, student editors read the papers and judged them on the basis of content, originality, grammar, historical research, documentation of primary sources, and clarity of presentation. All students received a grade reflective of their efforts, and those students whose papers were not accepted were encouraged nonetheless to help in the production of the journal. Papers selected were then returned to their authors along with suggested comments and corrections and the request for a complete rewrite. The authors then corrected their papers, retyped them and returned them to the editorial committee for final proofing, all within a two week period.

Upon completion of this task, a school district secretary was paid to type the articles in journal form on a word processor. An appropriate cover design and illustrations were drawn by members of the class to complement the various articles printed.

Numerous pictures culled from the historical society and personal photos were also included. All materials were then collated by the editorial committee and sent to the Assistant Superintendent for Instruction. At that point our Assistant Superintendent, who was most instrumental in seeing this project through to its conclusion, helped procure the necessary funds from the district and contracted the printing of the journal cover to a local printing firm. Copy machines in the district office were used to print the journal in order to keep costs down. The end result was the publication of Amityville Memorial High School's history journal, *The Journal of Historical Inquiry: Amityville, The First Half of the Twentieth Century.*

This was a tremendous undertaking. Many extra hours were spent helping students organize their ideas, make contacts for appropriate references, correct rough drafts and, of course, decide which papers were most suitable for publication in the journal. Making sure students kept to the timetable was another constant headache. The additional time devoted to editorial matters should not be overlooked either.

The local history journal's initial success was startling. Over two hundred copies were printed and distributed throughout the community. Another one hundred copies were printed to meet a growing demand. With that response in mind, I decided to continue student research in local history. The next journal issue dealt specifically with the World War II scene. Again local records, newspaper accounts, and in-depth oral interviews were employed by the students. What were some of the war experiences of Amityville's veterans and how did they readjust to civilian life? What did Amityville's women at home do during the war? What contributions did Amityville's Blacks make to the war effort? How did the churches, businesses, and veterans' organizations uphold local morale? What kinds of patriotic lessons were being taught in schools? These and many more questions were asked in order to ascertain the patriotic feeling of the community during World War II.

The 1985 volume, for instance, examines Amityville since 1945, a period in which the rapid impact of postwar suburbanization provided ample research material. Students probed the following topics in rich detail: the civil rights movement; physical changes in the village; the department of Public Works; effects of "the Amityville horror"; Bay life; village government; the history of the Amityville High School football team; expansion of the school system; and de facto segregation in the public schools.

The last volume published (1990) focused on group projects, accompanied by two individual papers. An institutional theme was proposed for this issue. Full-scale articles were written by teams that explored the history of South Oaks Hospital—a nationally known rehabilitation center, Bethel African Methodist Episcopal Church—Long Island's oldest African-American church, the development and economic impact of the Grand Old Hotels that dotted the village's seashore and attracted numerous tourists and visitors, the Amityville public school system and its evolution from the turn of the century to the present, the religious and educational training at Beth Sholom Center, and the social activities of the Amityville Masonic Lodge. The research and writing resulted in an impressive 160 page document.[5] Two of the essays are reproduced at the end of this article: "A History of the Bethel African Methodist Episcopal Church" and "Amityville: A Vacationland."

Elementary school teachers will delight in knowing that a colleague, Janet Perrin, and I recently published a local history text for third and fourth grade students attending the Amityville schools. Entitled *A Walk Through History: A Community Named Amityville* (Amityville, NY: Amityville School District, 1993), it was published with a competitive grant from the New York State Archives and Records Administration. The book was the direct product of the local history journals discussed in this article. The book's purpose is to call to the attention of Amityville elementary school students their community's historical roots and how it functions. What exactly is the role of communities in our society? The book is divided into sections for teachers and students. The teacher section presents an historical overview of the community in order of chronological development. The book is richly illustrated with documents and photographs from the village historical society. Chapters for students focus on the public schools, places of worship, life along the Great South Bay, and community services such as the police and fire departments. The chapter about famous village residents and visitors recalls a wide range of well-known individuals including: vaudevillian, Will Rogers; rifle expert, Annie Oakley; Eleanor Roosevelt, and Senator Joseph McCarthy—each of whom spoke from the stage of Amityville Memorial High School; and former New York State Governor Alfred E. Smith. An activities section is appended to the text for classroom use.

Part of the book is written from a multicultural perspective, in story fashion, narrated by a pair of fictional grandparents who take a tour of the Amityville community and recall their youthful experiences with their grandchildren by their side. Elementary school students will find the narrative interesting and informative. The elementary text would not have been possible were it not for the efforts of the Advancement Placement history journal project. Consequently, what started out as a high school assignment has conveniently found its way into the elementary school classroom.

Was the journal project worth the effort? Yes, indeed! Students involved in writing the articles, working as editors, drawing illustrations and seeking appropriate photos acquired a genuine feel for historical creativity and originality; they were making their community's past come alive through their own printed words. Most significantly, in working with primary sources they recognized the often overlooked fact that their subjects were real people and organizations, and that actual events remain an integral part of our history and are not simply "facts" appearing on pages glued together between two cardboard covers. In addition, by my emphasizing the publishing aspect, students took greater care in what they wrote, and they came to appreciate the quoted dictum in Barzun's *Teacher in America:* "The substances of what we think, though born in thought, must live in ink."[6]

With the publication of a student's local history journal an attempt has been made to help students learn to investigate and analyze historical evidence in a professional manner, write better essays, and appreciate the importance of hard editing necessary for publication. Bearing in mind these ideas, it is quite possible that we became many minds sharing one thought in recreating our local past.[7]

Notes

1. Jacques Barzun, *Teacher in America*, rev. ed. (Garden City, NY: Anchor Books, 1954), 31.

2. Paul L. Ward, *Elements of Historical Thinking*, rev. ed. (Washington, DC: American Historical Association, 1971), 5.

3. Ralph Adams Brown and William G. Tyrrell, *How to Use Local History* (Washington, DC: National Council for the Social Studies, 1966), 1–2, 7.

4. Wood Gray, et al, *Historian's Handbook: A Key to the Study and Writing of History* (Boston: Houghton Mifflin, 1964). This is an indispensable reference work commonly used by professional historians.

5. No volumes were published in 1988 or 1989; the 1990 volume was the last one produced to date. As a result of the Regents' Action Plan and budget cuts, the Advanced Placement senior elective in American history at Amityville High School was merged with an eleventh grade regents class. Students in the Edmund W. Miles Junior High School in Amityville produced a *History Journal* in 1990 and 1991 under the direction of William Kritz.

6. Barzun, 58.

7. Works on Amityville's history include the following: Mary Gangi, Grace Hughes, and Seth Purdy, *Looking Back at Amityville* (Amityville, NY: Amityville Historical Society, 1982); William T. Lauder, *Amityville Historical Revisited* (Amityville, NY: Amityville Historical Society, 1992); Cecil Ruggles, *Amityville Officers of the Law* (Amityville, NY: Amityville Historical Society, 1986); Seth Purdy, Jr. and Elodie Dobbins, *Amityville Remembers: A Pictorial History 1880–1920* (Amityville, NY: Amityville Historical Society, 1986); and William T. Lauder and Charles F. Howlett, *Amityville's 1894 School House* (Amityville, NY: Park Avenue School Centennial Committee, 1994).

Following are two examples of student work from the 1990 issue of the Amityville High School's *History Journal*. Copies of the 1984–1987 and 1990 issues of *The Journal of Historical Inquiry* and the elementary text, *A Walk Through History: A Community Named Amityville*, as well as 1990 and 1991 issues of Amityville's *Junior High School History Journal* are available in the Long Island Studies Institute. (Editor)

A History of the Bethel African Methodist Episcopal Church, Amityville*

Chemene Pelzer, La Wanda Rice, and Morgan Tucker

The origins of Bethel African Methodist Episcopal Church began in 1814 by Daniel Squires and Delancy H. Miller. Together these two men started a bible class holding regular sessions in local residents' homes. This small bible school later became known as the Bethel Sunday School. One year later Daniel Squires decided that the small town of Amityville was in need of a place for black residents to practice their faith. For the next fifteen years, church meetings were held in the homes of numerous church members, while still their small congregation continued to grow. In 1839 the congregation was deeded the site on the west side of Albany Avenue, just south of Great Neck Road. This contribution of religious faith and love was shown by Mr. and Mrs. Elias and Fanny Hunter.

In 1844 the congregation received as a gift an old icehouse to be used as the congregation's first house of worship. The first pastor of this church was Rev. Benjamin Bates, grandfather of the late Charles A. Holmes, a member of one of the church's founding families. As an example of his dedication to his church and its members, Rev. Bates, a resident of Jamaica, Queens, would make his weekly trek on foot to direct services in Amityville. This long trip was later much shortened when Rev. Bates was given a horse by the members of the church.

In 1850, the members of Bethel, Amityville saw their first official church built. Later, a carriage house was added on to the rear of the church. This building became a milestone in the history of our town as its first black church. The church was incorporated and became a member of the New York Conference of the African Methodist Episcopal Church. In 1866, Rev. Alexander Posey, whose beloved wife was buried in Payne Cemetery plotted directly across the street from the church, was the first pastor appointed on record.

---

*Reprinted from the Amityville Memorial High School's *History Journal* 1990.

Courtesy Amityville Historical Society
Bethel A.M.E. Church, c. 1890

Around the turn of the century the building was raised to add a lower auditorium to help expand the church. In 1904, a parcel of land was purchased for $100 and the church parsonage was built at Albany Avenue and Smith Street. This was done to help the resident pastor and his family because, in those times, a church pastor made only $36.00 as a yearly salary. In 1912, an official cornerstone was laid during an emotional ceremony for an enlarged building.

In 1925, Bethel A. M. E. founded the first all-black Boy Scout Troop of America. Mr. Charles A. Holmes, Mr. Nicolas Miller, and Mr. Alverne Mayhew were the organizers and first committeemen of the church scouts. For the first year or so, it was called Troop #2 but according to some of the older members of the troop that number was taken away and it was designated Troop #17. Their importance to the community increased dramatically during the years of World War II as they began selling War Bonds, collection drives, and going on into service in the Armed Forces when they became of age. Charles Bellinger, Ernest Hunter, Bill Brewster, Thomas Greener, Ralph Bean,

Wilbur, Milford, and Wellinton Devine, Richard Bellinger, Chris, Herb, and Louis Leftenant, Everett Collins, Sonny and Gordon Anderson, Nathan Arvon, James Collins, Edgar Scurlock, and Arthur Jackson were some of the boys to go through this troop on their way toward manhood.

Following World War II, farmland in Amityville gave way to new home developments, and the facilities of the old church became obsolete due to the arrival of many new residents. Those members who envisioned the future needs of the church began to formulate plans to expand in 1957 under the pastorship of Rev. C. B. Crawford. Ms. Martha Green Coster, then a member, deeded the present site at 20 Simmons Street, Copiague, to the community. It was abandoned and with the intercession of the late Mrs. Fowler Ross, it was passed on to the church.

There was strong objection to moving a portion of the congregation. It meant leaving their heritage. However, the decision was made and in 1957, a building fund drive began, led by the Rev. John W. Lee, and the church entered into a huge building fund campaign with earning $125,000 as their goal.

Great sacrifices had to be made on the part of the congregation. The parsonage was sold because Rev. Lee purchased his own home. Finally, on June 28, a ground breaking ceremony was held with the late Bishop George W. Baber, Prelate of the First Episcopal District, conducting. The first phase was over and the dedicated members prepared for another long struggle. In 1965, the old Bethel church burned. The Opportunity Center graciously opened their doors and they worshipped there until the new church was ready.

The very first service in the new church was a funeral, preceding the first worship service on March 12, 1967 in the lower auditorium. They later moved into the main sanctuary on Palm Sunday, March 19, 1967 on folding chairs and a donated pulpit stand. Sunday May 7, 1967 a consecration service was held by the late Rev. John D. Bright, Senior Bishop of the A. M. E. Church.

In 1969, under the leadership of Rev. Samuel C. Thornton, the church was furnished with new pulpit furniture. The cross and pews were donated by church members. From 1969 to 1972, the pastor at Bethel was Samuel Thornton. During his pastorship at the church, a piece of land across the street was purchased and a parsonage was erected. The present pastor currently resides there.

In 1972, Rev. Forrest Worton took over until 1974. Since its inception Bethel A. M. E. has prided itself on its ability to aid in the prosperity of the community its members lived in. In 1974, under the direction of Rev. Simon P. Bouie, Bethel Day Care Center opened its doors in an effort to help facilitate the phasing in of mothers back into the work force. In addition to this service, Mr. Charles Bellinger removed the cornerstone, bell, and cross from old Bethel and placed them in the new church's vestibule. Now, every Sunday, Bethel's members have the opportunity to enjoy the sounds of the tolling bell before and after worship services.

As proud African Methodists, the Restoration Committee was established to restore the Old Church. Since 1975 stained glass windows have beautified and enhanced the holy appearance of the Bethel Church. They were dedicated by families and auxiliaries of the church. On January 30, 1977, Bethel was fortunate enough to have a Rogers Providence 300 organ dedicated to it. In addition, the Bethel Church family sponsors a radio ministry which has expanded from half hour to one full hour of air time on radio station WNYG 1440 AM on Sundays from nine o'clock to ten o'clock A. M. It serves an ever increasing number of persons in hospitals, nursing homes, prisons, and others who are unable to be a part of a regular worship service.

Rev. Bouie's successor and Bethel's pastor is Rev. Floyd N. Black. Through Rev. Black's diligence, honesty, insight, and able leadership, Bethel A. M. E. has succeeded in decreasing heavy debts, given the privilege of a second mortgage burning and a new refurbished administrative wing. In July of 1983, the Bethel Scholarship Committee was organized. This fund was established to encourage youth in their scholastic endeavors.

In 1979, the old Bethel A. M. E. Church was added to the National Register of Historical Places by the United States Department of the Interior. Unfortunately, the church burned down in 1989. Bethel A. M. E. is now in the planning stages of erecting a community family access center on the site of their first church.

Strong conviction, courage, and faith have brought the Bethel Church thus far. Work was done by man, but their hands were guided by God. "On this Rock I will build my Church and the gates of Hell shall not prevail against it."

Amityville: A Vacationland*

Colleen Linehan and Beth Brice

VACATION—an interlude, usually of several days or weeks, from one's customary duties, as for recreation or rest; a holiday.

In the early twentieth century Amityville served as a vacationland. The village attracted many people, primarily businessmen and their families from urban areas, including Manhattan and Brooklyn. Perhaps Amityville became a resort town because of its access to the beach, splendid hotels, waterfront activities, impressive village, quaint houses, or simply the atmosphere of the "Friendly Bay Village."

A trip to Amityville began at Penn Station in New York City. Travellers would board a steam powered train and change in Jamaica for an Amityville bound train. Once they arrived in Amityville, they disembarked at Powell's Station.

Beginning in 1909, the passengers had the option to take the trolley to the southern points of Amityville. One of the trolleys ran from Amityville to Huntington and the other from Amityville to Babylon. For the price of a nickel, one could take the trolley to his final destination.

During the summer months there was a large influx of vacationers. The population of three hundred seemed to double during this period. This summer getaway began as a cluster of large summer houses located on Ocean Avenue. With the increase of popularity, more lodging became available as the hotels arose. These hotels also opened many job opportunities for the youths.

Small family hotels sprung up as well as grand hotels of great elegance located on the bay. The first hotel people saw as they approached the village was the Wardles Hotel. This was originally Kiernan's Hotel. It included twenty-five rooms, a large veranda, and a dining room. This hotel was popular among businessmen. This was in the heart of the village on Broadway and was convenient to the railroad station. Rates here were as low as ten dollars per week.

*Reprinted from the Amityville Memorial High School's *History Journal* 1990.

The next hotel seen while travelling down Broadway was the Amity Inn. This was located on the corner of Merrick Road and Broadway and was originally the Duryea Hotel. This inn contained twenty-five rooms and was very popular among cyclists. The Amity Inn also hosted the New York-Amityville bicycle race in 1899 (Purdy, Dibbins p. 32). The present bar, Crawdaddy's, now stands at the site of the Amity Inn.

The Nassau Inn could be seen on Merrick Road just west of County Line Road. "This was a popular hostelry for motorists travelling along Merrick Road" (Purdy, Dibbins p. 31).

During the Vanderbilt Cup Races, the Motor Parkway racers lodged at the Hotel Alexandria.

Located on the right side of Broadway near the railroad track was Wright's Hotel. This became an important place politically, as it was used to decide the county boundary line.

For water lovers there were a few hotels located on the Great South Bay. These were the Hotel New Point, Hathaway Inn, and the Narragansett Inn. These, however, were only open during the summer months.

The Hotel New Point seems to have been the most elegant of Amityville's hotels. It was the most stylish with the finest furnishings and most modern facilities. With its one hundred and

Courtesy Amityville Historical Society
New Point Hotel, Amityville, Long Island

fifty rooms, it could accommodate up to three hundred visitors. The cost was reasonable at $12.50 a week. This price included use of its own private beach, bath house, and dining room. Entire families used to stay there with their horse, carriage, and driver. The meals were also rated exceptional as the fishermen sold their days catch to them. "In the winter, local youths could be found roaming the premises illegally" (interview with Ruggles).

When rooms here were not available, people went to the Hathaway Inn. This was across the street and to the north of the New Point. Sixty rooms were available here. Visitors spent time on Hathaway's veranda. Sailing, crabbing, swimming and relaxing were all part of a stay at the Hathaway.

Both the Hotel New Point and the Hathaway Inn were built in the 1890s and were found at the end of Grand Central Avenue.

The last of the waterfront hotels was the Narragansett Inn. This was located at the end of Ocean Avenue and was operated by Carl Fuchs, Sr.

Fire Island has always brought tourists to Long Island. The barrier beaches provide excellent summer outings. Many of the people who came to stay at the hotels of Amityville would spend their days at the beaches.

Courtesy Amityville Historical Society
Hathaway Inn, Amityville, Long Island

Transportation to the beaches was either by boat or ferry. Beginning in 1905, Amityville provided three picturesque ferry boats to the public; the Adele, the Atlantic, and the Columbia. "They sailed from docks along the Amityville Creek to Hemlock Beach and later to Gilgo Beach" (Lauder p. 3). Sometimes they would travel to High Hill Beach or Oak Island Beach.

"The Adele was built, owned and operated by Charles Sprage" (Lauder p. 4). "The Atlantic and Columbia were both built, owned, and operated by Frank Wicks" (Lauder p. 4). The Atlantic was built purposely for ferry use, although the Columbia was not. It was a cat boat that Wicks converted into a ferry.

After boarding the ferry, it would travel out of the creek into the bay, on its way passing small islands. The last sight on the right would be the Narragansett Inn on Ocean and Richmond. The ferry would travel on to its destination, Hemlock Heading.

The passengers would disembark and enjoy their day at the beach and Van Nostrand's Pavilion. "The Pavilion provided a dining room, porches, and bath houses for visitors" (Lauder p. 5). It was a necessity to have a bowl of Becky Van Nostrand's famous clam chowder. The Van Nostrand's worked throughout the year to prepare for the summer.

In 1910 a destructive storm carved an inlet through the beach and nearly ruined the Pavilion. From that point on, Hemlock Beach became less popular and the people spent time at Gilgo Beach as an alternative. At Gilgo, two beach pavilions, similar to Van Nostrand's were used by beachgoers. Islanders and vacationers from the city all came to Amityville and made use of the ferries and beautiful beaches until 1928. Among the vacationers were many famous people including Fred Stone, Will Rogers, Al Capone, and Annie Oakley. Stone, an actor, and Rogers, a roper, purchased houses on Clocks Blvd. and could often be seen playing polo throughout Amityville. Capone organized a baseball team at the Amityville High School. Oakley, who travelled with Buffalo Bill, spent her time demonstrating her good shot to the men of Amityville.

The summers of the early 1900s were a monumental time in the history of Amityville. The events and people of that era shall never be forgotten.

Bibliography

Dibbins, Elodie and Seth Purdy Jr. *Amityville Remembered: A Pictorial History, 1880–1920*. Amityville: Amityville Historical Society, 1984.

Dibbins, Elodie, Seth Purdy, Jr., and Cecil H. Ruggles. *A Backward Glance*. Amityville: Amityville Historical Society, 1980.

Lauder, William T. "Ferry Boats From Amityville to the Outer Beach." *Newsletter Amityville Historical Society* (Summer 1982): 2–5.

Powell, Charles S. "Hemlock Beach." *Historical Supplement* (1987): 1–4.

Saxton, Walter A. "Change at Jamaica." *Newsletter Amityville Historical Society* (Fall 1981): 2–7.

Whalen, John. "Went the Trolley." *Amityville Record* (December 19, 1984): 5.

"A Visit to Amityville, 1910." Filmstrip. Marlene and David Thomas.

Interview with *Seth Purdy*, January 1990.

Interview with *Cecil Ruggles*, April 27, 1990.

Interview with *Roy and Peggy Van Nostrand*, April 21, 1990.

Resources and Bibliographies

Natalie A. Naylor

This reference section provides guides, resources, and bibliographies for exploring Long Island history. In addition to general suggestions for research and recommended reading, there are specialized bibliographies on Long Island's Indians, African Americans, women, arts and artists, and books geared to younger readers. Lists of audio-visual resources, important Long Islanders, nationally notable Long Island women, historical societies, historic houses and museums, a chronology, and population statistics are provided. The brief introduction in this first section identifies some of the most important resources.

Introduction to Resources for Exploring Local History

You should begin at the local public library for publications on your community, town, county, or Long Island and read one or two of these first. Consult the "Guide to Resources," "Selected Reading on Long Island History," and specialized bibliographies of interest below.

Every municipality (whether county, city, town, or incorporated village) has an historian charged with the preservation of town records and history. Most have limited funds and time restrictions; telephone or visit to see what assistance can be provided.

Many communities have historical societies. Some, as well as other historical organizations, provide benefits to members, educational services, and resources. A few of the larger historical organizations in Nassau and Suffolk counties are listed here; see also the list of historical societies below. The dues listed are for individual memberships in 1994 and may change; most have different categories of membership. Museums are often a good source for resources, information, programs, and publications; see separate listing.

Organizations

The Friends for Long Island's Heritage is a support group for the Nassau and Suffolk County museums. Membership benefits include reduced or free admission to county museums, discounts at museum shops, and lower rates for the *Long Island Forum*. Membership dues are $25-$50; for information call 571-7617; 1864 Muttontown Rd., Syosset, NY 11791.

The Long Island Archives Conference (LIAC) is dedicated to improving the quality of archives and providing professional care for documents. Holds fall and spring conferences and workshops; issues newsletter three times a year; dues $10. Information: Peggy McMullen, 718-990-6734.

The Long Island Studies Council (LISC) includes academic, avocational, and public historians who meet monthly at Hofstra or at museum sites for informal programs. Newsletter includes events and exhibits on Long Island and information on new publications. LISC reprinted H. Girard's "Needles and Thread: Jewish Life in Suffolk County" ($1). Membership dues are $10; information (c/o LISI), 463-5846.

The Long Island Studies Institute (LISI) is a collaboration between Hofstra University and Nassau County. The reference collection, located at 619 Fulton Ave., Hempstead (Hofstra's West Campus), is open to the public for the study of Long Island local and regional history weekdays from 9-5 (to 4 Fridays in the summer). Barbara Kelly is Curator, 463-6409. The Institute sponsors conferences and publications; contact Natalie Naylor, Director, 463-5846 or 463-6411.

The Nassau County Historical Society has five meetings a year with speakers and publishes a *Journal* annually. Dues are $10; Box 207, Garden City, NY 11530; 735-4783.

The Society for the Preservation of Long Island Antiquities (SPLIA) is concerned with preserving the built environment of historical significance, including historic homes, mills, and work places. SPLIA maintains several historic properties and a gallery with changing exhibits in Cold Spring Harbor (367-6295). It publishes *Preservation Notes* and sponsors other publications. Robert B. MacKay is Executive Director, 93 North Country Rd., Setauket, NY 11733; 941-9444. Membership is $25.

The Suffolk County Archaeological Association (SCAA) extends to and includes Nassau County. SCAA's goals include conserving and properly studying prehistoric sites on Long Island, providing a program of public education and publications, building a more responsible attitude toward cultural resources on Long Island, and sponsoring proper archaeological digs. Dues are $20; P.O. Drawer 1542, Stony Brook, 11794-3323; 929-8725.

The Suffolk County Historical Society has a museum with permanent and changing exhibits, a research library, and genealogical workshop. The Weathervane Shop has an excellent collection of books and materials on local history and genealogy. Membership dues are $25 which include the quarterly *Register.* The Society is located at 300 West Main Street, Riverhead 11901; 727-2881.

Periodicals

Back issues are available at many libraries; they are valuable sources of information on diverse topics.

The Long Island Forum began as a monthly in 1938; now published by the Friends for Long Island's Heritage, since 1987 it has been a quarterly. Copies of current issues are available at Old Bethpage Village Restoration or by subscription. Editor, Richard Welch; subscription information, 571-7600, fax 571-7623.

The Long Island Historical Journal has been published twice a year (spring and fall) since 1988; a subscription is $15 a year. Roger Wunderlich, Editor; Department of History, SUNY at Stony Brook, Stony Brook, NY 11794-4348; 632-7500.

The Nassau County Historical Society Journal has been published since 1937. Originally published quarterly, it is now issued annually. A subscription is included with membership in the Society ($10, Box 207, Garden City 11530); back issues are available from the museum shop at Old Bethpage Village Restoration. Editors: Myron H. Luke, Natalie A. Naylor, and Edward J. Smits.

Publications

Long Island: A Guide to New York's Suffolk and Nassau County by Raymond Spinzia, Judith Spinzia, and Kathryn Spinzia is an excellent guidebook with extensive information listing historic sites, museums, nature conservancies, parks, sites on the National Register, and Tiffany windows. Hippocrene Books published a revised edition in 1991. See also *Where to Go and What to Do on Long Island* by SCOPE (Dover Press, 1993).

Guide to Resources on Long Island Studies*

Natalie A. Naylor

The local public library is usually the best place to begin looking for information on a specific community's history. It is advisable to consult the vertical file as well as the card catalog; also, some books may only be in the children's section and separately catalogued. A few libraries have their Long Island books in a special room which may have more limited hours. A telephone call is recommended to check hours, especially for the Long Island collections. Historical societies may have valuable resources, also. Some societies charge a nominal fee of $2-$3 or $5 daily for non-members to use their collection.

The Reference and Adult Services Division (RASD) of the Suffolk County Library Association published *A Guide to Local History Collections in Suffolk County* in 1983. This study was based on a survey of public, museum, historical society, and religious libraries and provides a useful overview of the scope of local history resources. The Long Island History Committee of RASD has compiled a helpful list of "Local History Resource People in Suffolk County Public Libraries" (1990, 1993).

Some libraries have specialized Long Island collections with maps, atlases, newspapers, clippings, photographs, oral histories, family records, government documents, genealogies, and manuscripts as well as published books and pamphlets.

Among the libraries with strong Long Island collections:

Brooklyn (formerly Long Island) Historical Society, 128 Pierrepont Street, Brooklyn, 11201; fee; (718) 624-0890, fax 875-3869.

Bryant Library, Local History Collection, Paper Mill Road, Roslyn 11576; (516) 621-2240, fax 621-7211.

East Hampton Free Library (Pennypacker Collection), 159 Main Street, East Hampton, 11937; (516) 324-0222.

Freeport Memorial Library, West Merrick Road and South Ocean Avenue, Freeport, 11520; (516) 379-3274; fax 868-9741.

Glen Cove Public Library, Robert R. Coles Long Island History Room, Glen Cove Avenue, Glen Cove, 11542; (516) 676-2130, fax 676-2788.

---

*Updated from *Evoking a Sense of Place*, ed. Joann P. Krieg, (Interlaken, NY: Heart of the Lakes Publishing, 1988), 173-7.

Great Neck Library, Bayview Avenue at Grist Mill Lane, Great Neck, 11024; (516) 446-8055, fax 829-8297.

Hempstead Public Library, 115 Nichols Court, Hempstead, 11550; (516) 481-6990, fax 481-6209

Hicksville Public Library, 169 Jerusalem Avenue, Hicksville, 11801-4999; (516) 931-1417, fax 822-5672.

Hofstra University, see Long Island Studies Institute.

Huntington Historical Society, Research Library, 209 Main Street, Huntington, 11743; nominal fee to use; (516) 427-7064, fax 427-7056.

Huntington Public Library, 338 Main Street, Huntington, 11743; (516) 427-5165, fax 673-3351.

Long Island Historical Society, see Brooklyn Historical Society.

Long Island Studies Institute, Hofstra University Special Collections, West Campus, 619 Fulton Avenue, Hempstead, 11550-4575; (516) 463-6409, 6411, or 6417, fax 463-6438.

Longwood Public Library, Thomas R. Bayles Collection, Middle Country Road, Middle Island, 11953; (516) 924-6400, fax 924-7538.

Manhasset Public Library, 30 Onderdonk Avenue, Manhasset, 11030; (516) 627-2300, fax 627-4339.

Middle Country Public Library, 101 Eastwood Boulevard, Centereach, 11720; (516) 585-9393, fax 585-6541.

Middle Island, see Longwood Public Library.

Nassau County Museum Collection; see Long Island Studies Institute.

Patchogue-Medford Library, Long Island Collection, 54-60 East Main Street, Patchogue, 11772; (516) 654-4700, fax 289-3999.

Port Washington Public Library, 245 Main Street, Port Washington, 11050; (516) 883-4400, fax 944-6855.

Queens Public Library, Long Island Collection, 89-11 Merrick Blvd., Jamaica, 11432; (718) 990-0770, fax (718) 658-8312.

Rockville Centre Public Library, Historical Collection and Archives, 221 North Village Avenue, Rockville Centre, 11570; (516) 766-6257, fax 766-6090.

Roslyn, see Bryant Library.

Setauket, Emma S. Clark Library, Capt. Edward R. Rhodes Memorial Collection of Local History, 120 Main Street, Setauket, 11733; (516) 941-4080, fax 941-4541.

Smithtown Library, Long Island Room, Richard H. Handley Collection, 1 North Country Road, Smithtown, 11787; (516) 265-2072 x38, fax, 265-5945.

Suffolk Community College, Long Island History, 533 College Road, Selden, 11784; (516) 451-4172, fax 451-4697.

Suffolk County Historical Society, Research Library, 300 West Main Street, Riverhead, 11901; nominal fee; (516) 727-2881.

SUNY Stony Brook, Frank Melville, Jr. Memorial Library, Department of Special Collections, SUNY Stony Brook, Stony Brook, 11794-3323; (516) 632-7119.

Westbury Library and Historical Society of the Westburys, Long Island collection in the "Cottage," 454 Rockland Street, Westbury, 11590; (516) 333-0176.

Hofstra University Library resources on Long Island Studies are described in greater detail, not only to acquaint researchers with this particular library, but to familiarize them with the types of sources useful for research in Long Island Studies. Other libraries may have similar types of materials.

Most of the Long Island materials are located in the Long Island Studies Institute in Hofstra University's Special Collections. The Institute collections are on the second floor of the Library Services Center, 619 Fulton Avenue (Hempstead Turnpike, Route 24), one-half mile west of the main Hofstra campus, next to Twin Oaks residence facility; parking is adjacent to the building. The Long Island Studies Institute was created by Hofstra University and Nassau County in 1986. It includes the Nassau County Museum collection (formerly located in Eisenhower Park, East Meadow), and Hofstra's James N. MacLean Nassau County American Legion Memorial collection of New York State and Long Island History. The Institute is open Monday-Friday, 9–5 (Friday 9–4 during summer months).

The Long Island Studies Institute has virtually all the published histories of Long Island and its communities, many biographies and genealogies of Long Islanders, periodicals on Long Island history, and other regional histories. In addition to monographs on Long Island and New York State, there is an extensive collection of unpublished doctoral dissertations on Long Island history. (Ask to see the "Bibliography of Dissertations on Long Island History" and other specialized bibliographies at the Institute.) The photograph collection, numbering approximately 12,000, is outstanding. Most are copied with negatives and indexed by place, subject, and person; the card file includes a small copy of the photograph. More than a hundred different newspapers are available on microfilm—three eighteenth-century New York City papers and Long Island papers from the 1820s to the present. Most of the papers were published in Queens or Nassau County, but there are some Suffolk papers as well. The *Brooklyn Eagle* is available to 1925. A published 1983 index lists the newspapers alphabetically, chronologically (by decades), and by the village or town. (See also updated lists of newspaper holdings.)

The vertical file of clippings and other uncatalogued materials is arranged according to place, topic, or individuals; the 42 file drawers are particularly strong in Nassau County materials. The map collection (approximately 800 items) includes atlases, geological survey maps, road maps, photostats, and original maps of Long Island. Census materials include: the U.S. manuscript census 1790–1900 for Queens, Nassau, and Suffolk counties, Nassau and Suffolk for 1910–1920; New York indexes for federal censuses, 1790–1850; New York State manuscript census for Long Island, 1915 and 1925; and bound volumes of some New York special censuses (e.g. Census of Agriculture, 1850, 1860). Nassau County telephone books from 1913–date are available on microfilm. Other primary soures include Queens County estate inventories and deeds (1789–1898 with index, on microfilm), and more than 100,000 archival and manuscript items, including e.g., Carman and other family papers, records of the Queens County Agricultural Society, Civil War Enrollment Books (Hempstead), Nassau County Poll lists (1850s–1860s, 1900–1911), and account books.

Information pertinent to Long Island Studies also can be found in the Joan and Donald E. Axinn Library at Hofstra. The Reference department on the first floor of the Axinn Library, for example, has publications of the Long Island Regional Planning Board and Nassau County Planning Commission, as well as the United States Census. The Periodicals Department (ground floor) has the *Nassau County Historical Society Journal* (1937–date), *Long Island Forum* (1938–date), *Journal of Long Island History* (1961–1982), and *Long Island Courant* (1965–1968), as well as other journals which may have articles on Long Island (e.g. *de Halve Maen* and *New York History*). Elementary and secondary school textbooks and curriculum guides are in the Curriculum Materials Center (ground floor). Government Documents (ground floor) has Geological Survey maps, vital statistics, and census data. Archives (on the first floor, Library Services Center, West Campus) has Hofstra University records, but also, for example, audio tapes of some Hofstra radio station programs dealing with Long Island.

The Long Island Studies Institute also collects films and media dealing with Long Island. In addition to tapes of programs it has sponsored, it has copies of audio tapes of talks at Suffolk County Historical Society's Genealogical and History meetings; see the bibliography below of Audio-Visual Resources.

The best collections of books in print on Long Island are available at the museum shops at the Suffolk County Historical

Society (SCHS) in Riverhead, the SPLIA Gallery, in Cold Spring
Harbor, and Old Bethpage Village Restoration. The Weathervane
Gift Shop of the SCHS periodically publishes a book list which
serves as a mail order catalog.

Inexpensive reproductions of maps from the 1873 Beers' *Atlas
of Long Island, New York* are available at the museum shops
operated by the Friends for Long Island's Heritage (e.g. at Garvies
Point and Old Bethpage). These facsimiles show roads, houses,
and property owners for local communities or sections of towns
in 1873. The SCHS has available for sale attractive handpainted
reproductions of 1873 maps of many communities from the
Nelson Studio.

Historical societies and organizations are another important
resource. Most publish newsletters, pamphlets, or journals; many
have regular meetings with programs; some operate museums
or historic houses. See separate lists of historical societies and
museums below. Information about quarterly meetings of the
Association of Suffolk County Historical Societies can be obtained
from the Suffolk County Historical Society, (516) 727–2881. The
Association of Nassau County Historical Organizations
(ANCHO) prints a leaflet with information on its member
societies. The Long Island Museum Association (LIMA) has
published a guide for Nassau and Suffolk museums. The Long
Island Studies Institute periodically issues a newsletter.

By New York State law, every village, city, and town is
required to have an officially appointed historian. Although the
resources available to them vary greatly, these historians are
usually very knowledgeable about their area. Contact the
municipality (village, town, or city) to learn who is the appointed
historian for the community. The Nassau County Historian is
Edward J. Smits, (Nassau Hall, 1864 Muttontown Road, Syosset,
11791, 516-571–7600) and J. Lance Mallamo is the Suffolk County
Historian and Director of Historic Services for Suffolk County
(PO Box 144, West Sayville, 11796; 516–854–4970). They should
be able to provide information on other local historians and
historical organizations. The Queens Historical Society (143–35
37th Avenue, Flushing 11547; 718-939–0647), and Brooklyn
Historical Society (128 Pierrepont St., Brooklyn 11201;
718-624–0890), can provide information on their counties. See
also section on Historical Societies below.

Selected Reading on Long Island History

Natalie A. Naylor

This is revised and updated from the bibliography which appeared in *Evoking a Sense of Place*, ed. Joann P. Krieg (Interlaken, NY: Heart of the Lakes Publishing, 1988), 178–82. It includes thematic or general histories but omits most histories of local communities and biographies of famous Long Islanders.

Adams, James Truslow. *History of the Town of Southampton*, 1918. Reprint; Port Washington: I. J. Friedman, 1962.

American Institute of Architects, Long Island Chapter and The Society for the Preservation of Long Island Antiquities (hereafter, SPLIA). *AIA Architectural Guide to Nassau and Suffolk Counties, Long Island*. New York: Dover, 1992.

Bailey, Paul. *Long Island: A History of Two Great Counties*. New York: Lewis Publishing, 1949. 3 vols.

Berbrich, Joan D. *Three Voices From Paumanok: The Influence of Long Island on James Fenimore Cooper, William Cullen Bryant, Walt Whitman*. Port Washington: I. J. Friedman, 1969.

Bertomen, Michele. *Transmission Towers on the Long Island Expressway: A Study of the Language of Form*. New York: Princeton Architectural Press, 1992.

Boegner, Peggie Phipps and Richard Gachot. *Halcyon Days: An American Family Through Three Generations*. New York: Old Westbury Gardens and Abrams, 1987. The Phipps family of Old Westbury Gardens.

Bookbinder, Bernie. *Long Island: People and Places, Past and Present*. New York: Harry Abrams, 1983.

Breen, T. H. *Imagining the Past: East Hampton Histories*. Reading, MA: Addison-Wesley, 1989.

Cagney, W. Oakley. *The Heritage of Long Island*. Port Washington: I. J. Friedman, 1970. Includes woodcuts of historic houses and buildings.

Capozzoli, Mary Jane. *Three Generations of Italian-American Women in Nassau County, New York, 1925-1981*. New York: Garland, 1990.

Caro, Robert. *The Power Broker: Robert Moses and the Fall of New York*. New York: Alfred A. Knopf, 1974. Chapters 9, 11-13, and 17 focus on Long Island roads and parks; see also J. Krieg, ed., *Robert Moses* (1988).

Cole, John N. *Striper, A Story of Fish and Man*. Boston: Little, Brown, 1978.

---

* In print, 1994.

Cray, Robert E., Jr. *Paupers and Poor Relief in New York City and Its Rural Environs, 1700-1830.* Philadelphia: Temple University Press, 1988.

Dade, George, and Frank Strnad. *Picture History of Aviation on Long Island, 1908-1938.* New York: Dover, 1989.
int, 1994.

Dobriner, William M. *Class in Suburbia.* Englewood Cliffs, NJ: Prentice Hall, 1963. Chapters on Levittown and Huntington.

Dunwell, Steve. *Long Island: A Scenic Discovery.* [Dublin, NH]: Foremost, 1985. This is an example of a "coffee-table" book with contemporary color photographs and minimal text; other titles of this type are not been included.

Dyson, Verne. *Anecdotes and Events in Long Island History.* Port Washington: I. J. Friedman, 1969.

_____. *The Human Side of Long Island.* Port Washington: I. J. Friedman, 1969.

Edwards, Everett, and Jeanette Rattray, 1932. *Whale-off: The Story of American Shore Whaling.* Reprint; New York: Coward and McCann, 1956.

Estes, John. *Hampton Style: Houses, Gardens.* New York: Little Brown, 1993.

Failey, Dean F. *Long Island Is My Nation: The Decorative Arts and Craftsmen, 1640-1830.* Setauket: SPLIA, 1976. A revised edition is planned.

Ferguson, Eleanor. *My Long Island.* Las Vegas, NV: Scrub Oak Press, 1993. Reminiscences by Hal Fullerton's daughter; see Sachs, *Blessed Isle.*

Frankenstein, Alfred. *William Sidney Mount.* New York: Harry N. Abrams, 1975.

Funnel, Bertha H. *Walt Whitman on Long Island.* Port Washington: Kennikat, 1971.

Gabriel, Ralph H. *The Evolution of Long Island: A Story of Land and Sea,* 1921. Reprinted; Port Washington: Ira J. Friedman, 1960.

Goldberger, Paul. *The Houses of the Hamptons.* New York: Knopf, 1986.

Goody, Susan Rabbit. *Woven History: The Technology and Innovation of Long Island Coverlets, 1800-1860.* Setauket: SPLIA, 1992.

Guild Hall Museum. *The Artist as Teacher: William Merritt Chase and Irving Wiles.* Exhibit catalog, 1994.

Hamilton, Harlan. *Lights and Legends: A Historical Guide to the Lighthouses of Long Island Sound, Fishers Island Sound, and Block Island Sound.* Stamford, CT: Westcott Cove, 1987.

Heffner, Robert J. *Windmills of Long Island.* New York: SPLIA and W.W. Norton, 1983.

Horne, Field, ed. *The Diary of Mary Cooper: Life on a Long Island Farm, 1768-1773.* Oyster Bay: Oyster Bay Historical Society, 1981.

Hummel, Charles F. *With Hammer in Hand: The Dominy Craftsmen of East Hampton, New York.* Charlottesville: University Press of Virginia, 1968.

Jackson, Birdsall. *Stories of Old Lond Island*. Rockville Centre: Paumanok Press, 1934.

Keeler, Robert F. *Newsday: A Candid History of the Respectable Tabloid*. New York: Arbor House/Morrow, 1990.

Kelly, Barbara M. **Expanding the American Dream: Building and Rebuilding Levittown*. Albany: State University of New York, 1993.

Kelly, Barbara M. ed. **Long Island: The Suburban Experience*. Interlaken, NY: Heart of the Lakes Publishing for the Long Island Studies Institute [hereafter HLP/LISI], 1990.

Ketcham, Diane E. *Long Island: Shores of Plenty*. Chatsworth, CA: Windsor, 1988.

Krieg, Joann P. **Long Island and Literature*. Interlaken, NY: HLP/LISI, 1989.

____, ed. **Evoking a Sense of Place*. Interlaken, NY: HLP/LISI, 1988.

____, ed. **Long Island Architecture*. Interlaken, NY: HLP/LISI, 1991.

____, ed. **Robert Moses: Single-Minded Genius*. Interlaken, NY: HLP/LISI, 1989.

LaGumina, Salvatore J. **From Steerage to Suburb: Long Island Italians*. New York: Center for Migration Studies, 1988.

____, ed. *Ethnicity in Suburbia: The Long Island Experience*. [Garden City: Nassau Community College], 1980.

Lieberman, Janet E. and Richard K. Lieberman. *City Limits: A Social History of Queens*. Dubuque, IA: Kendall/Hunt, 1983.

Lightfoot, Frederick S., Linda B. Martin, and Bette S. Weidman. **Suffolk County, Long Island in Early Photographs, 1867-1951*. New York: Dover, 1984.

Long Island Forum, 1938-date; see especially 50th Anniversary issue, Spring 1988 with reprinted articles. Published monthly to 1987; now quarterly.

Long Island Historical Journal, 1988-date; published bi-annually by SUNY Stony Brook.

Luke, Myron H. **Vignettes of Hempstead Town, 1643-1800*. Hempstead: LISI, 1993. Included also in *Roots and Heritage of Hempstead Town*, ed. Natalie A. Naylor (1994).

Luke, Myron H. and Robert Venables. *Long Island in the American Revolution*, Albany: New York State American Revolution, Bicentennial Commission, 1976.

MacDermott, Charles J. *Suffolk County, N.Y.* New York: James H. Heineman, 1965.

MacKay, Robert B., Geoffrey L. Rossano, and Carol A. Traynor, eds. *Between Ocean and Empire: An Illustrated History of Long Island*. Northridge, CA: Windsor, 1985.

Malley, Richard C. **In their Hours of Ocean Leisure: Scrimshaw in the Cold Spring Harbor Whaling Museum*. Cold Spring Harbor: Whaling Museum, 1993.

Mallory, Leoniak and Jane S. Gombieski. **To Get the Vote: Woman Suffrage Leaders in Suffolk County*. Town of Brookhaven, 1992.

Manley, Seon. *Long Island Discovery: An Adventure into the History, Manners, and Mores of America's Front Porch*. Garden City: Doubleday, 1966.

Marcus, Grania. *A Forgotten People: Discovering the Black Experience in Suffolk County*. Setauket: SPLIA, 1988.

Marhoefer, Barbara. *Witches, Whales, Petticoats, and Sails: Adventures and Misadventures from Three Centuries of Long Island History*. Port Washington; Kennikat, 1971.

Marshall, Bernice Schultz. *Colonial Hempstead: Long Island Life Under the Dutch and English*, 1937 (under Bernice Schultz). Reprint, 2d ed.; Port Washington: I. J. Friedman, 1962. Includes towns of Hempstead and North Hempstead.

Matthiessen, Peter. **Men's Lives: The Surfmen and Baymen of the South Fork*. New York: Random House, 1986. Paperback edition does not include photographs.

McCormick, Larry. **Living with Long Island's South Shore*. Durham, NC: Duke University Press, 1984.

Miller, Marvin D. **Wunderlich's Salute: The Interrelationship of the German-American Bund, Camp Siegfried, Yaphank, LI, and the Young Siegfrieds*. Smithtown: Malamud-Rose, 1963.

Moss, Richard Shannon. **Slavery on Long Island: A Study in Local Institutional and Early Communal Life, 1609-1827*. New York: Garland, 1993.

Murphy, Robert C. **Fish-Shape Paumanok: Nature and Man on Long Island*, 1964. Reprint; Great Falls, VA: Waterline Books, 1991.

Nassau County Historical Society Journal, 1937-date; currently published annually.

Naylor, Natalie A. ed. **Exploring African-American History*. Hempstead: LISI, 1991.

——. **Roots and Heritage of Hempstead Town*. Interlaken: HLP/LISI, 1994.

Naylor, Natalie A., Douglas Brinkley, and John Allen Gable, eds. **Theodore Roosevelt: Many-Sided American*. Interlaken, NY: HLP/LISI, 1992.

Newman, Tobie and Sylvia Landow, ed. **That I May Dwell Among Them*. Syosset: Conference of Jewish Organizations of Nassau County, 1992.

Oakley, Helen McK. *Christopher Morley on Long Island*. Roslyn: The Christopher Morley Knothole Association, 1967. See also Oakley's biography of Morley, *Three Houses for Lunch* (1976).

Overton, Jacqueline. *Long Island's Story*, 1932. 2nd ed. with sequel, by Bernice S. Marshall. Port Washington: I. J. Friedman, 1961.

Palmedo, Philip and Edward Beltrami. **The Wines of Long Island: The Birth of a Region*. Great Falls, VA: Waterline Books, 1993.

Parrish Art Museum. **The Long Island Country House, 1870-1930*. Southampton: The Parrish Art Museum, 1988.

Pellegrino, Charles R. and Joshua Stoff. *Chariots for Apollo: The Making of the Lunar Module*. New York: Atheneum, 1985.

Pennypacker, Morton. *George Washington's Spies on Long Island and New York*. Brooklyn: Long Island Historical Society, 1939. Also, *Supplement*.

Pisano, Ronald G. **A Leading Spirit in American Art: William Merritt Chase, 1849-1916*. Seattle: University of Washington Press, 1983.

____. *Long Island Landscape Painting, 1820-1920*. Boston: Little, Brown, 1985.

____. *Long Island Landscape Painting*, Vol. II: *The 20th Century*. Boston: Little, Brown, 1990.

____. *Summer Afternoons: Landscape Paintings of William Merritt Chase*. New York: Little Brown, 1993.

Puleston, Dennis. *A Nature Journal: A Naturalist's Year on Long Island*. New York: W. W. Norton, 1992.

Randall, Monica. *The Mansions of Long Island's Gold Coast*, 1979. Rev. ed.; New York: Rizzoli, 1987.

Rattray, Jeanette Edwards. *Ship Ashore! A Record of Maritime Disasters off Montauk and Eastern Long Island, 1640-1955*. New York: Coward-McCann, 1955.

Ross, Peter and William S. Pelletreau. *A History of Long Island From its Earliest Settlement to the Present Times*. 3 vols. New York: Lewis Publishing, 1902.

Sachs, Charles E. *The Blessed Isle: Hal B. Fullerton and His Image of Long Island, 1897-1927*. Interlaken, NY: LISI and Suffolk County Historical Society, 1991. See also Ferguson, *My Long Island*.

Sclare, Liisa, and Donald Sclare. *Beaux-Arts Estates: A Guide to the Architecture of Long Island*. New York: Viking Press, 1980.

Schmitt, Frederick. *Mark Well the Whale! Long Island Ships to Distant Seas*. 2d ed. Cold Spring Harbor, NY: Whaling Museum Society, 1986.

SCOPE [Suffolk County Organization for the Promotion of Education], *Where to Go and What to Do on Long Island*. New York: Dover, 1993.

Seyfried, Vincent. *Queens: A Pictorial History*. Norfolk, VA: Donning, 1982.

Seyfried, Vincent F. and William Assadorian *Old Queens N.Y. in Early Photographs*. New York: Dover, 1990.

Shodell, Elly. *In the Service: Workers on the Grand Estates of Long Island, 1890's-1940's*. Port Washington, NY: Port Washington Library, 1991.

——. *Cross Currents: Baymen, Yachtsmen, and Long Island Waters, 1830s-1990s*. Port Washington: Port Washington Library, 1993.

Smith, Mildred H. *Early History of the Long Island Railroad, 1834-1900*. Uniondale: Salisbury Printers, 1958.

Smits, Edward J. *Nassau: Suburbia, U.S.A.* Syosset: Friends of Nassau County Museum, 1974.

Sobin, Dennis P. *Dynamics of Community Change: The Case of Long Island's Declining "Gold Coast."* Port Washington, NY: Ira J. Friedman, 1968.

Solomon, Nancy. *On the Bay: Bay Houses and Maritime Culture on Long Island's Marshlands*. Syosset: Friends for Long Island's Heritage, 1992.

Spinzia, Raymond, Judith Spinzia, and Kathryn Spinzia. *Long Island: A Guide to New York's Suffolk and Nassau Counties*, 1988. Rev. ed.; New York: Hippocrene Books, 1991.

Stayton, Kevin L. *Dutch by Design: Tradition and Change in Two Historic Brooklyn Houses*. New York: Phaidon Universe, 1990. The Schenck houses in the Brooklyn Museum.

Stevens, William. *Discovering Long Island*. New York: Dodd, 1939.

Stoff, Joshua. *The Aerospace Heritage of Long Island*. Interlaken: HLP/LISI, 1989. See also his *From Airship to Spaceship* (1991) and *From Canoes to Cruisers* (1994) for younger readers.

——. *The Thunder Factory: The History of the Republic Aviation Corporation*. 1990.

Stoff, Joshua and William Camp. *Roosevelt Field, World's Premier Airport*. Terre Haute, IN: SunShine House, 1992.

Stone, Gaynell, and Donna Ottusch-Kianka, eds. *The Historical Archaeology of Long Island: The Sites*. Stony Brook: Suffolk County Archaeological Association, 1985.

Stott, Peter H., ed. *Long Island; An Inventory of Historic Engineering and Industrial Sites*. U.S. Dept of Interior and SPLIA, 1974.

Tarleton, Diane Bennett and Linda Tarleton. *W. C. Bryant in Roslyn*. Roslyn: The Bryant Library, 1978.

Taylor, Lawrence. *Dutchmen on the Bay: The Ethnohistory of a Contractual Community*. Philadelphia: University of Pennsylvania Press, 1983. West Sayville.

Thompson, Benjamin. *History of Long Island From Its Discovery and Settlement to the Present Time*. 3 vols. 1839-1849, 1918. Reprint; Port Washington: I. J. Friedman, 1962.

Tredwell, Daniel M. *Personal Reminisences of Men and Things on Long Island*. 2 vols. Brooklyn: C. A. Ditmas, 1912-17.

Tulin, Miriam. *The Calderone Theatres*. Hempstead: Long Island Studies Institute, 1991.

Turner, John. *Exploring the Other Island: Seasonal Guide to Nature on Long Island*. Great Falls, VA: Waterline Books, 1994.

Vagts, Christopher R. *Suffolk: A Pictorial History*. Huntington, NY: Huntington Historical Society, 1983.

Valentine, Harriet. *The Window to the Street*, 1981. Reprint; Cold Spring Harbor: Whaling Museum, 1991. Helen Rogers' 1840s diary.

Valentine, Harriet G. and Andrus T. Valentine. *An Island's People: One Foot in the Sea, One on Shore*. Huntington: Privately printed, 1976.

Van Liew, Barbara Ferris. *Long Island Domestic Architecture of the Colonial and Federal Periods: An Introductory Study*. Setauket, NY: SPLIA, 1974. Originally published in *Nassau County Historical Society Journal* 33 (1973): 1-27; revised and enlarged in SPLIA pamphlet.

Viemeister, August. *An Architectural Journey Through Long Island*. Port Washington: Kennikat Press, 1974.

Watson, Elizabeth L. *Houses for Science: A Pictoral History of the Cold Spring Harbor Laboratory*. Plainview: Cold Spring Harbor Laboratory Press, 1991.

Weidman, Bette S., and Linda B. Martin. *Nassau County, Long Island in Early Photographs, 1869-1940*. New York: Dover, 1981.

Weigold, Marilyn. *The American Mediterranean: An Environmental, Economic, and Social History of Long Island Sound.* Port Washington, NY: Kennikat, 1974.

Welch, Richard. **Memento Mori: The Gravestones of Early Long Island, 1680-1810.* Syosset, NY: Friends for Long Island's Heritage, 1984. See also his 1986 **Guide* to Long Island graveyards.

———. **An Island's Trade: Nineteenth-Century Shipbuilding on Long Island.* Mystic, CT: Mystic Seaport Museum, 1993.

Williamson, W. M. **Adriaen Block: Navigator, Fur Trader, Explorer, New York's First Shipbuilder, 1611-13.* New York: Museum of the City of New York, 1959. Pamphlet.

Wilson, Rufus Rockwell. *Historic Long Island*, 1902. Reprint; Port Washington, NY: Ira J. Friedman, 1972.

Wunderlich, Roger. **Low Living and High Thinking at Modern Times.* Syracuse: Syracuse University Press, 1992. The 19th century anarchist community at Brentwood.

Wyckoff, Edith Hay. *The Fabled Past: Tales of Long Island.* Port Washington: Kennikat, 1978.

Younger, William Lee. **Old Brooklyn in Early Photographs, 1865-1929.* New York: Dover, 1978.

Ziel, Ron. **The Long Island Rail Road in Early Photographs.* New York: Dover, 1990.

Ziel, Ron, and George H. Foster. **Steel Rails to the Sunrise: LIRR*, 1965. Rev. ed.; Mattituck: Ameron House, 1987.

Ziel, Ron and Richard Wettereau. **Victorian Railroad Stations of Long Island.* Bridgehampton: Sunrise Special Ltd., 1988.

Zim, Larry, Mel Lerner, and Herbert Rolfes. *The World of Tomorrow: The 1939 World's Fair.* New York: Harper and Row, 1989.

For more extensive and specialized bibliographies (e.g., on Native Americans, women, authors, architecture, African Americans, and artists), see other bibliographies in this book and in: *Long Island and Literature,* by Joann P. Krieg, 43-4; *Long Island Architecture,* edited by Joann P. Krieg, 159-61; *Exploring African-American History,* edited by Natalie A. Naylor, 13-20, 29-30, 46, 55, 60-3; and *Roots and Heritage of Hempstead Town,* edited by Natalie A. Naylor, 233-41. For articles, see Natalie A. Naylor, "Recent Articles on Long Island History," *Long Island Historical Journal* 6 (Fall 1993): 106-20 and indexes to *Long Island Forum* and *Nassau County Historical Society Journal.*

The best selection of local history books in print is at the museum shops at the Suffolk County Historical Society in Riverhead (Weathervane, 300 W. Main St.; 516-727-2881), SPLIA Gallery in Cold Spring Harbor (516-367-6295), St. James General Store (516 Moriches Road; 516–862–8333), and Old Bethpage Village Restoration (516-572-8415).

References and Resources: Long Island

Bibliographies and Reference Works

Bunce, James E. and Richard P. Harmond, eds. *Long Island as America: A Documentary History.* Port Washington: Kennikat, 1977.

Gerard, Helene. *Discovering Long Island History,* 1983. $5. Available from Suffolk County Historical Society (SCHS).

Hoff, Henry B., ed. *Long Island Source Records: From "The New York Genealogical and Biographical Record."* Baltimore: Genealogical Publishing, 1987.

Middle Country Public Library. *Long Island Bibliography,* 1984.

Naylor, Natalie A. "Recent Articles on Long Island History." *Long Island Historical Journal,* 6 (Fall 1993): 106-20.

Onderdonk, Henry, Jr. *Revolutionary Incidents of Suffolk and Kings Counties,* 1849. Reprint; Port Washington: Kennikat, 1970.

——. *Revolutionary Incidents of Queens County* [including present-day Nassau County], 1846. Reprint; Port Washington: Kennikat, 1970.

Peterson, Jon A., ed. *A Research Guide to the History of the Borough of Queens.* Queens: History Department, CUNY, Queens College, 1987.

Proehl, Karl H. and Barbara Shupe. *Long Island Gazetteer: A Guide to Current and Historical Place Names.* Bayside: LDA Publications, 1984.

Sealock, Richard B., and Pauline A. Seely. *Long Island Bibliography.* Baltimore, MD: Edwards, 1940.

Seversmith, Herbert F. and Ken Stryker-Rodda. *Long Island Genealogical Source Materials: A Bibliography.* Washington, DC: National Geneological Society, 1962.

Shaver, Peter D. *The National Register of Historic Places in New York State.* New York: Rizzoli, 1993. Listing of properties by counties includes brief information on architect, style, history of sites: Kings is 69-75; Nassau, 89-93; Queens, 132-4; and Suffolk, 155-62.

Spinzia, Raymond, Judith Spinzia, and Kathryn Spinzia. *Long Island: A Guide to New York's Suffolk and Nassau Counties,* 2nd ed., 1991. Includes lists of Tiffany windows and sites on the National Register as well as museums, historic sites, parks and preserves.

SUNY Stony Brook Library and Long Island Regional Planning Board, *Historical Population of Long Island Communities, 1790-1980,* 1982. Decennial census data.

Tooker, William. *Indian Place Names on Long Island and Islands Adjacent,* 1911. Reprint; Port Washington: Ira J. Friedman, 1962.

Willensky, Elliot and Noraval White. *AIA Guide to New York City.* 3d ed. New York: Harcourt Brace Jovanovich, 1988. Brooklyn and Queens, 564-797.

---

* In print, 1994.

Maps

Beers, *Atlas*. Facsimile reproductions of 1873 maps of communities. Available at museum shops at Garvies Point and Old Bethpage; $1.25. Suffolk County Historical Society and SPLIA Gallery have handpainted 1873 maps from Nelson Studio (751-0447).

Colton, "1852 Map of Long Island," Library of Congress, $13.50 for 8-1/2"x22" copy.

"Geological Survey Map of Long Island," 1842. Facsimile reproduction of large map. John Martino, 49 Brookhill Lane, Huntington, 11743; 368-8174 or 212-242-7650; $10.25.

"Historical Map of Long Island," decorative 20"x27"; Charles W. Smith Co. (802 Upper Gulph Rd., Wayne, PA 19087; $7.95); OBVR and SCHS.

No company currently produces a large Long Island wall map; Graphic Learning has a laminated map and Nystrom has desk maps of Long Island. Road maps can be used, as well as the maps in the local Community Telephone Directory. Reproductions of old maps are very useful. OBVR and SCHS may have other maps.

Posters and Multi-Media Resources

Museums at Stony Brook. *Nineteenth-Century Music and Dance in the Art of William Sidney Mount*, 1986. Slides, tapes, activity sheets, teacher's guide; $150. Grades 2-8. The Museums, 1208 Route 25A, Stony Brook 11790; 751-0066.

Newsday in Education, "Long Island/Community Studies," available to teachers ordering *Newsday* for classes. Teacher's handbook, student booklets, 4-foot map, copies of historical articles, and audio visual resources; 843-2181.

Parrish Art Museum. Slide-sound kits on William Merritt Chase, Fairfield Porter, "People, Places, and Things," and Regional Architecture of the South Fork; can be borrowed, gr. 7+ (25 Job's Lane, Southampton 11968; 283-2118).

Society for the Preservation of Long Island Antiquities (SPLIA), *The Style of Long Island—300 Years of Architecture and the Decorative Arts*, 1987. Poster (24"x36") with pictures of 117 buildings and artifacts. Available ($8.50) from SPLIA (93 N. Country Rd. Setauket, 11773; 941-9444) or at their Gallery in Cold Spring Harbor. Also "Long Island African American Heritage," 2x3-foot map, photos and biographical information on individuals; $5.

Suffolk County Archaeological Association (SCAA). "Native Long Island" map, 23"x37" with Indian place names and sites; brief text and "Native Technology," 26"x39" poster on material culture of Indians. Each $13; available from SCAA, P.O. Drawer 1542, Stony Brook, NY 11790; 929-8725; they are also at SCHS.

Suffolk County Explorer, 1992. An interactive videodisk; BOCES III (884-1000 x230; Karla Reiss or Alan Walker).

See also separate listing of films and videos in bibliography of Audio-Visual Resources below.

Books on Long Island History for Younger Readers

Natalie A. Naylor

Many of these books should be available in the school or public library, though most of the older titles are now out-of-print. A history of your local community may be available, though few have been written for children. Some of the books listed were published privately or by historical societies (full publication information may be in other bibliographies in this book). The Weathervane Shop at the Suffolk County Historical Society (300 W. Main Street, Riverhead 11901; 727-1881), the museum shops at Old Bethpage Village Restoration (572-8415), the SPLIA Gallery in Cold Spring Harbor (Main Street at Shore Road; 367-6295), and the St. James General Store (516 Moriches Rd., St. James 11780; 862-8333) have good resources on local history.

Bailey, Paul. *Historic Long Island in Pictures, Prose, and Poetry*, 1956.
Carpenter, Angelica and J. Shirley. *Frances Hodgson Burnett: Beyond the Secret Garden*, 1990.
Cobblestone, "Voice of Walt Whitman," 7 (May 1986), 5 (no. 586); see also issues of *Cobblestone* listed in "Resources and Guides for Local History" below, though they are not specifically Long Island. Grades 4-7.
Cooney, Barbara. **Hattie and the Wild Waves: A Story from Brooklyn*, 1990. Fiction.
Deutsch, Babette. *Walt Whitman, Builder for America*, 1941.
Farrell, Vivian. **Robert's Tall Friend: A Story of the Fire Island Lighthouse*, 1987. Fiction. Gr. 4-7.
Foster, John. *The Gallant and Gray Trotter*, 1974. Fiction ("Lady Suffolk").
Gerard, Helene. *Needles and Thread: Jewish Life in Suffolk County*, 1982/1986.
Gibbs, Alonzo. *By a Sea-Coal Fire*, 1968. Fiction.
Halsey, Carolyn. **Colonial Life on Long Island*, 1957/1986. Privately printed. Gr. 3-6; 22 pp.
Homire, Marion Hunt Berg. *Grandmother Burned Peachpits*, 1972. Reminiscences of growing up on an East Meadow farm in the early 20th century (contact Three Village Historical Society, Box 76, East Setauket 11733; 751-3730). Gr. 4+, 62 pp.

---

* In print, 1994.

Howard, Nancy Shroyer. *William Sidney Mount: Painter of Rural America.* Worcester, MA: Davis, 1994.
Huntington Historical Society. *Street Sleuths! Learning to Look at Buildings,* 1987. Gr. 6, 20 pp.
Long Island Forum, 1938-date. Published monthly until 1987; now a quarterly. Good 4th readers could use some articles.
Kittredge, Mary. **Barbara McClintock, Biologist,* 1991.
Marhoeffer, Barbara. *Witches, Whales, Petticoats and Sails,* 1971.
Overton, Jacqueline. *Long Island's Story,* 1929. Reprinted, 1962 with additions by Bernice Marshall.
Stoff, Joshua. **From Airship to Spaceship: Long Island in Aviation and Spaceflight,* 1991. Gr. 4+
_____. **From Canoes to Cruisers: The Maritime Heritage of Long Island,* 1994. Gr. 4+.
Society for the Preservation of Long Island Antiquities. **Learning to Look at Architecture,* 1991. 12 pp.
Turner, Glennette Tilley. **Lewis Howard Latimer,* 1991.
Voelbel, Margaret. *The Story of an Island: The Geology and Geography of Long Island,* 1963.
Yeaton, Sam. *A Natural History of Long Island,* 1972.

Native American Indians

Bailey, Paul. **The Thirteen Tribes of Long Island,* 1959/1982. Gr. 7+, 25 pp.
Lowey, Warren. *Little Fox, Indian Boy,* 1972. Fiction.
Grumet, Robert S. **The Lenapes,* 1989. Indians in western Long Island were Lenapes. Gr. 8+.
Halsey, Carolyn. **The Indians of Long Island,* 1986. Privately printed. Gr. 3-6, 24 pp.
Kraft, Herbert C. **The Lenape Indians of New Jersey,* 1987. Gr. 4; western Long Island Indians were Lenape.
Overton, Jacqueline. *Indian Life on Long Island,* 1938/1975. Gr. 4+, 150 pp.
Truex, James and Gaynell Stone. **A Way of Life: Indians of Long Island, Prehistoric Period,* 1985. Gr. 5+, 14 pp.
Van Laan, Nancy. **Rainbow Crow,* 1989. Retelling of a traditional Indian story. Gr. 5-9.
Wilbur, C. Keith. **The New England Indians,* 1978. (Includes Indians on eastern Long Island.) Gr. 7+.
_____. **Indian Handicrafts,* 1990.

Revolutionary War

Berleth, Richard. *Samuel's Choice,* 1990. Fiction.
Blakeless, Katherine and John. "The Culper's Secret Ink," pp. 87-101 in *Spies of the Revolution,* 1962.
Burchard, Peter. *Whaleboat Raid,* 1977. Fiction.
Currie, Catherine. **Anna Smith Strong and the Setauket Spy Ring.* Privately printed, 1990.

Forman, James. *The Cow Neck Rebels,* 1969. Gr. 7-9.
Groh, Lynn. *The Culper Spy Ring,* 1969. Gr. 5+
Halsey, Carolyn. **The Revolution on Long Island,* 1987. Gr. 3-6. 24 pp.
Haynes, Betsy. *Spies on the Devil's Belt,* 1974. Fiction. Gr. 5-8.
Jones, Peter. *Rebel in the Night,* 1971. Fiction.
Lancaster, Bruce. *The Secret Road,* 1962. Fiction on the Culper spy ring.
Lee, Susan and John. *The Battle for Long Island and New York,* 1975. 48
     pp.
Mantel, S. J. *Tallmadge's Terry,* 1965. Fiction. Gr. 4-8.
Marhoefer, Barbara. *Eye Witness, 1776,* 1976.
McGee, Dorothy. *Sally Townsend, Patriot,* 1952. Fictionalized
     biography.
Orton, Helen Fuller. *Hoof-beats of Freedom,* 1936. Fiction. Gr. 5-8.

Theodore Roosevelt (limited to books in print)

Beech, James. **Theodore Roosevelt: Man of Action,* 1991.
Cobblestone; the March 1993 issue is devoted to Theodore Roosevelt.
Fritz, Jean. **Bully for You, Teddy Roosevelt!* 1991. Highly recommended.
     Gr. 7+.
Kent, Zachary, **Theodore Roosevelt,* 1988. Also, **The Story of the Rough
     Riders,* 1991.
Markham, Lois. **Theodore Roosevelt,* 1985.
McCafferty, Jim. **Holt and the Teddy Bear,* 1991.
Monjo, F. N. **The One Bad Thing About Father,* 1970/1987. Fictionalized
     biography.
Parks, Edd W. **Teddy Roosevelt: All-Round Boy,* 1989.
Quakenbush, Robert. **Don't You Dare Shoot That Bear,* 1984/1990.
Sabin, Lou. **Teddy Roosevelt, Rough Rider,* 1986.
Sandak, Cass R. **The Theodore Roosevelts,* 1991.
Stefoff, Rebecca. **TR: 26th President of the United States,* 1988.
Weitzman, David. **The Mountain Man and the President,* 1993. John
     Muir and TR.
Whitelaw, Nancy. **Theodore Roosevelt Takes Charge,* 1992.

Pictorial Books.

Although written for adults, these books can be used by
younger readers.

American Institute of Architects and the Society for the Preservation
     of Long Island Antiquities. **AIA Architectural Guide to Nassau and
     Suffolk Counties, Long Island,* 1992.
Cagney, W. Oakley. *The Heritage of Long Island,* 1970.
Dade, George and Frank Strnad. **Picture History of Aviation on Long
     Island, 1908-1938,* 1989.
Gillon, Edmund V., Jr. **Cut & Assemble: Early American Buildings at Old
     Bethpage Village Restoration,* 1990.

Kramer, Frederick A. *Long Island Rail Road: A Pictorial Record of the Steam-to-Diesel Transition East of Jamaica,* 1986.

Lewis, Cyril A. *Historical Long Island Paintings and Sketches,* 1964.

Lightfoot, Frederick S., Linda B. Martin, and Bette S. Weidman. **Suffolk County, Long Island in Early Photographs, 1867-1951,* 1984.

Morrison, David D. *Long Island Rail Road: Steam Locomotive Pictorial.*

New York State Retired Teachers Association, Long Island Zone. *Old Schoolhouses: Nassau and Suffolk Counties,* 1976.

Seyfried, Vincent F. and William Assadorian. **Old Queens, NY in Early Photographs,* 1990.

Smith, M. H. **Garden City, Long Island in Early Photographs, 1869-1919,* 1987.

Solomon, Nancy et al. **On the Bay: Bay Houses and Maritime Culture on Long Island's Marshlands,* 1992.

Viemeister, August. *An Architectural Journey Through Long Island,* 1974.

Weidman, Bette S. and Linda B. Martin. **Nassau County, Long Island in Early Photographs, 1869-1940,* 1981.

Younger, William Lee. **Old Brooklyn in Early Photographs, 1865-1929,* 1990.

Ziel, Ron. **The Long Island Rail Road in Early Photographs,* 1990.

_____ and Richard Wettereau. **Victorian Railroad Stations of Long Island,* 1988.

_____ and George Foster. **Steel Rails to the Sunrise: Long Island Rail Road,* 1952/1987.

Zorn, Peter A., Jr. with Eugene F. Provenzo, Jr. and Asterie B. Provenzo. **Cut & Assemble Lindbergh's "Spirit of St. Louis,"* 1992.

Textbooks

Hallock Farm. *Life in Mid-19th Century: A Primer for Local History,* 1984.

Lyons, Beth, with Noel Gish. **Long Island Then and Now,* 1989. Gr. 4.

Mannello, George. *Our Long Island,* 1964/1984. Gr. 7.

Sesso, Gloria and Regina White. **The Long Island Story,* 1992. Gr. 4.

Bibliography: Long Island Art and Artists

Melissa Patton and Natalie A. Naylor

AIA Architectural Guide to Long Island. Long Island Chapter of the American Institute of Architects and the Society for the Preservation of Long Island Antiquities [hereafter SPLIA]. New York: Dover, 1992.

Armstrong, Janice Gray, ed. *Catching the Tune: Music and William Sidney Mount.* Stony Brook, NY: The Museums at Stony Brook, 1987.

Ashton, Dore. *American Art since 1945.* New York: Oxford University Press, 1982.

Atkinson, D. Scott and Nicolai Cikovsky, Jr. *William Merritt Chase: Summers at Shinnecock 1891-1902.* Washington, DC: National Gallery of Art, 1987.

Brooklyn Museum. *Elias Pelletreau: Long Island Silversmith and His Sources of Design.* Brooklyn: The Brooklyn Museum, 1959.

_____. *Brooklyn before the Bridge: American Paintings from the Long Island Historical Society.* Brooklyn: The Brooklyn Museum, 1982.

Corbett, Cynthia Arps. *Useful Art: Long Island Pottery.* Setauket, NY: SPLIA, 1985.

Cornish, Alison. *Edward Lange Revisited.* Setauket, NY: SPLIA, 1990.

Currier Gallery of Art, Manchester, NH. *Jane Freilicher,* 1986. Exhibition catalog.

Doty, Robert, ed. *Jane Freilicher: Paintings.* New York: Taplinger Publishing, 1986.

Downes, Rackstraw. *Fairfield Porter: Art in Its Own Terms.* New York: Taplinger Publishing, 1979.

Duncan, Alastair. *Masterworks of Louis Comfort Tiffany.* New York: Harry N. Abrams, 1989.

East Hampton Center for Contemporary Art, East Hampton, NY. *Crosscurrents: The New Generation, 1990.* Exhibition catalog.

Failey, Dean F. "Elias Pelletreau: Long Island Silversmith." M.A. thesis, University of Delaware, 1971. (Copy in Long Island Studies Institute, Hofstra University.)

_____. *Long Island Is My Nation: The Decorative Arts and Craftsmen, 1640-1830.* Setauket, NY: SPLIA, 1976. Revised edition planned.

Failey, Dean F., and Zachary N. Studenroth. *Edward Lange's Long Island.* Setauket, NY: SPLIA, 1979.

Fairfield Porter. Boston: Museum of Fine Arts, 1982.

Fasanella, R. Marc. "The Environmental Design of Jones Beach State Park: Aesthetic and Ecological Aspects of the Park's Architecture

* Originally published under the title "Long Island Artists, Artisans, and Architecture" in *Long Island's History and Cultural Heritage* by Natalie A. Naylor, Patricia Snyder, and Melissa Patton (Southampton: Parrish Art Museum, 1992), 61-63; some titles have been added.

and Landscape." Ph.D. dissertation, New York University, 1991. (Copy in Long Island Studies Institute.)

Frankenstein, Alfred. *William Sidney Mount*. New York: Harry N. Abrams, Inc., 1975.

_____. *Painter of Rural America: William Sidney Mount*. Stony Brook, NY: The Museums at Stony Brook, 1968.

Goldberger, Paul. *Houses of the Hamptons*. New York: Alfred A. Knopf, 1986.

Grey Art Gallery, New York University. *Krasner/Pollock: A Working Relationship, 1981*. Exhibition catalog. Essay by Barbara Rose.

Guild Hall, East Hampton, NY. *East Hampton: The American Barbizon, 1850-1990*, 1969.

_____. *East Hampton Architecture: The Message of Its History*, 1979.

_____. *Alfonso Ossorio, 1940-1980*, 1980.

_____. *Artists and East Hampton: A 100-Year Perspective*, 1981.

_____. *Childe Hassam, 1859-1935*, 1981.

_____. *Thomas Moran: A Search for the Scenic*, 1981.

_____. *Poets and Artists of the Region Collaborating*, 1982.

_____. *Larry Rivers, Performing for the Family: An Exhibition of Paintings, Sculpture, Drawings, Mixed Media Works, Films and Video, 1951-1981*, 1983.

_____. *Long Island Modern: The First Generation of Modernist Architecture on Long Island, 1925-1960*, 1987.

_____. *En Plein Air: The Art Colonies at East Hampton and Old Lyme, 1880-1930*, 1989.

_____. *East Hampton Advant-Garde: A Salute to the Signa Gallery, 1957-1960*, 1990.

_____. *The Artist as Teacher: William Merritt Chase and Irving Wiles*, 1994.

Hall, Lee. *Elaine and Bill [de Kooning]: Portrait of a Marriage*. New York: Harper Collins, 1993.

Harrison, Helen A. "On the Floor." *Long Island Historical Journal* 3 (Spring 1991): 155-66. Re the floor in the former studio of Jackson Pollock, now part of Pollock-Krasner Museum and Study Center.

Hefner, Robert J., ed. *East Hampton's Heritage: An Illustrated Architectural Record*. New York: W. W. Norton, 1982.

_____. *Windmills of Long Island*. New York: W. W. Norton, 1983.

Hecksher Museum, Huntington, NY. *Fairfield Porter: Retrospective Exhibition*, 1974.

_____. *Arthur Dove and Helen Torr: The Huntington Years*, 1989. Exhibition catalog. Essay by Anne Cohen De Pietro.

_____. *Long Island Painters and Portraits*, 1981.

Hummel, Charles F. *With Hammer in Hand: The Dominy Craftsmen of East Hampton, New York*. Charlottesville, VA: University Press of Virginia, 1968.

Hunter, Sam. *Larry Rivers*. New York: Rizzoli International Publications, 1989.

Johnson, Deborah J. *Shepherd Alonzo Mount: His Life and Art*. Stony Brook, NY: The Museums at Stony Brook, 1988

Kenny, Peter, Frances Gruber Safford, and Gilbert T. Vincent. *American Kasten: The Dutch-Style Cupboards of New York and New*

Jersey, 1650-1800. New York: The Metropolitan Museum of Art, 1991.

Koch, Robert. Louis C. *Tiffany, Rebel in Glass.* New York: Crown Publishers, 1982.

Koppelman, Connie. "Back to Nature: The Tile Club in the Country." *Long Island Historical Journal* 3 (Fall 1990): 75-88.

Krieg, Joann P., ed. *Long Island Architecture.* Interlaken, NY: Heart of the Lakes Publishing, 1991.

Kroessler, Jeffrey A., and Nina S. Rappaport. *Historic Preservation in Queens.* Sunnyside, NY: Queensborough Preservation League, 1990.

Lewis, Cyril A. *Historical Long Island: Paintings and Sketches.* Westhampton Beach, Long Island Forum, 1964.

Long Island Landmarks. New York State Office of Planning Coordination, 1969.

Lyons, Lisa, and Robert Storr. *Chuck Close.* New York: Rizzoli International Publications, 1987.

MacKay, Robert B., ed. *Long Island Country Houses and Their Architects, 1860-1940.* Forthcoming from W. W. Norton.

Mendel Art Gallery, Saskatchewan, Canada. *Eric Fischl: Paintings,* 1985. Exhibit catalog. Essays by Bruce W. Ferguson, et al.

Modern Masters Series. New York: Abbeville Press. Concise studies on individual artists: de Kooning, Lichtenstein, Pollock, Warhol, and others.

Museum of Modern Art, New York. *Lee Krasner: A Retrospective,* 1983. Exhibition catalog. Essay by Barbara Rose.

Naifeh, Steven, and Gregory White Smith. *Jackson Pollock: An American Saga,* 1989. Reprint; New York: Harper Perennial, 1991.

Nassau County Museum of Fine Art, Roslyn, NY. *Abstract Expressionists and Their Precursors,* 1981. Exhibition catalog.

_____. *Long Island Sound Steamboats,* 1984. Essay by Edwin Dunbaugh.

_____. *Louis Comfort Tiffany: The Laurelton Years,* 1986.

Oldenbusch, Carolyn. "Long Island on Stone: Nineteenth Century Lithographs." *Long Island Forum* 57 (Summer 1994): 21-33.

Parrish Art Museum, Southampton, NY. *William Merritt Chase in the Company of Friends,* 1979.

_____. *17 Abstract Artists of East Hampton: The Pollock Years, 1946-56,* 1980.

_____. *The Long Island Landscape, 1865-1914: The Halcyon Years,* 1981.

_____. *American Paintings from The Parrish Art Museum,* 1982.

_____. *The Long Island Landscape, 1914-1946: The Transitional Years,* 1982.

_____. *The American Painter-Etcher Movement,* 1984.

_____. *Painting Naturally: Fairfield Porter and His Influences,* 1984.

_____. *Drawing on the East End,* 1988.

_____. *The Long Island Country House, 1870-1930,* 1988.

_____. *Painting Horizons: Jane Freilicher, Albert York, April Gornik,* 1989.

Pisano, Ronald G. *Charles Henry Miller: The Artistic Discoverer of the Little Continent of Long Island.* Exhibit catalog. Stony Brook, NY: The Museums at Stony Brook, 1979.

_____. *William Merritt Chase*. New York: Watson-Guptill Publications, 1979.

_____. *A Leading Spirit in American Art: William Merritt Chase, 1849-1916*. Seattle: University of Washington Press, 1983.

_____. *Long Island Landscape Painting, 1820-1920*. Boston: Little, Brown and Co., 1985.

_____. *Long Island Landscape Painting, II: The Twentieth Century*. Boston: Little, Brown and Co., 1990.

Pisano, Ronald G. and Alicia Longwell. *Photographs from the William Merritt Chase Archives*. Southampton: Parish Art Museum, 1992.

Poli, Bruce. *Suffolk County: A Place in Time*. Exhibition catalog; photographs celebrating Suffolk's Tercentenary. Riverhead, NY: Suffolk County, 1983.

Ross, Clifford, ed. *Abstract Expressionism: Creators and Critics, an Anthology*. New York: Harry N. Abrams, 1990.

Sclare, Liisa, and Donald Sclare. *Beaux-Arts Estates: A Guide to the Architecture of Long Island*. New York: Viking Press, 1980.

Shapiro, David. *Art for the People: New Deal Murals on Long Island*. Exhibition catalog. Hempstead, NY: Emily Lowe Gallery, Hofstra University, 1978.

Solomon R. Guggenheim Museum, New York. *Willem de Kooning in East Hampton*. 1978. Exhibition catalog. Essay by Diane Waldman.

Spinzia, Judith A. "Artistry in Glass: Louis Comfort Tiffany's Legacy in Nassau County." *Nassau County Historical Society Journal* 46 (1991): 9-17.

Spinzia, Raymond E., Judith A. Spinzia, and Kathryn E. Spinzia. *Long Island: A Guide to New York's Suffolk and Nassau Counties*. Rev. ed.; New York: Hippocrene Books, 1991. Includes information on Tiffany windows on Long Island, *passim* and 438-46.

Stayton, Kevin L. *Dutch by Design: Tradition and Change in Two Historic Brooklyn Houses, The Schenck Houses at The Brooklyn Museum*. New York: The Brooklyn Museum and Phaidon Universe, 1990.

Trupin, Bennett. *Elias Pelletreau, 1726-1820: Goldsmith of Southampton*. [Hallandale, FL: n.p.], 1984.

Van Lieu, Barbara Ferris. *Long Island Domestic Architecture of the Colonial and Federal Periods: An Introductory Study*. Setauket, NY: SPLIA, 1974. Reprinted and revised from article in *Nassau County Historical Society Journal* 33 (1973): 1-27.

Viemeister, August. *An Architectural Journey through Long Island*. Port Washington, NY: Kennikat Press, 1974.

William Sidney Mount. Stony Brook, NY: The Museums at Stony Brook, 1983.

William Merritt Chase: Summers at Shinnecock, 1891-1902. Videotape, 26 min. Washington, DC: National Gallery of Art, 1987.

W. M. Davis, 1829-1920: Port Jefferson's Foremost Painter. Port Jefferson, NY: Historical Society of Greater Port Jefferson, 1973.

Ziel, Ron and Richard Wettereau. *Victorian Railroad Stations of Long Island*. Bridgehampton, NY: Sunrise Special Ltd. Publishing, 1988.

Zilezer, Judith. *Willem de Kooning*. New York: Rizzoli, 1993.

Audio-Visual Resources

Part I is limited to films and videos which can be purchased or are available in libraries (locations are indicated). Most focus on Long Island, but a few are general local history guides (for example those produced by the American Association of State and Local History or the New York State Historical Association). Unless 16 mm. is specified, these are one-half inch videotapes; some commercial 16 mm. films can now be purchased in video format. See also Part II, "Additional Audio-Visual Resources in the Long Island Studies Institute," which includes resources which are not commercially available, but are available for viewing in the Institute. (As indicated, many of the videos in Part I are also in the Institute.)

Abbreviations and Sources

AASLH - American Association of State and Local History, 530 Church St., #600, Nashville, TN 37219; 615-255-2971, fax 615-255-2979.

HU - Hofstra University, Media Services, Axinn Library, Room 125 (west wing); 516-463-5986 (can be viewed, but not loaned).

LILCO - Long Island Lighting Company. LILCO Community Relations (516-545-5292) has made available videotapes for free rental to schools through Modern Talking Picture Service, 5000 Park Street North, St. Petersburg, FL 33709; 800-243-6877, fax 813-546-9323.

LISI - Long Island Studies Institute, Hofstra University-West Campus; 619 Fulton Ave., Hempstead, NY 11550; 516-463-6411. Can be viewed at the Institute.

LIVP - Long Island Video Project, c/o Madonia, 7 Oakcrest, Farmingville, NY 11738; 516-736-1943.

NLS - Nassau Library System (films and videos available through member libraries).

NYSHA - New York State Historical Association, PO Box 800, Cooperstown, NY 13326; 607-547-2533, fax 607-547-5384.

PBS - Public Broadcasting System, 1320 Braddock Place, Alexandria, VA 22314; fax 703-739-5269.

SCLS - Suffolk Cooperative Library System (videos available through member libraries).

SUNY-SB - State University of New York, Stony Brook, Frank Melville Library; AV, 632-7100 (available through interlibrary loan).

Part I: Films and Videos

Age of Aquaculture, The, 1971. 16 mm., 17 min. NLS.

A. T. Stewart's Garden City, 1994. 100 min. John Ellis Kordes (516-742-4113). Garden City's history decade by decade, from its origins to the 1990s. LISI.

Autumn Flight, 1966. 16 mm., 15 min. NLS. Migrating birds.

Battle of Long Island. 30 min. Revolutionary war battle in Brooklyn. Intercollegiate Video. SCLS.

Baymen, The, 1972. 16 mm., 15 min. Nassau County Museum. NLS, SUNY-SB; video in SCLS.

Baymen: Our Waters Are Dying, 1976. 16 mm., 29 min. NLS, SUNY-SB; video in SCLS.

Beacons in the Night: Long Island Lighthouses, 1987. 18 min. LIVP. LISI, SCLS.

Bright Legacy: The Story of Lewis Latimer, 1988. 27 min. Unitarian-Universalist Association (25 Beacon St., Boston 02108). Black inventor who lived in Flushing. LISI.

Brookhaven Spectrum, 1967. 16 mm., 15 min. Science research at Brookhaven National Laboratory. SCLS.

Brooklyn Bridge, 1982. 58 mins. Direct Cinema. HU, NLS.

Campaign American Style, 1968. 16 mm., 39 min. The 1968 Eugene Nickerson vs. Sol Wachtler race for county executive; CBS News. NLS.

Celebrating Teddy, 1973. 16 mm., 15 min. Biography produced by National Park Service.

Clipper Ships, 1974. 16 mm., 7 min. Aviation history, particularly 1939 seaplanes, in Port Washington. NLS.

Corner in Wheat, A, 1909. 16 mm., 10 min. D. W. Griffith's film; farm scenes filmed in Jamaica, Queens. NLS.

Coney Island, 1990. 58 min. PBS: American Experience. LISI.

Conversation with a Blacksmith, 1987. 22 min. LIVP. LISI, SCLS.

Crops Protected, Water Threatened, 1982. 20 min. Pesticide pollution of aquifer. Cornell University. A-V Resource Center.

Dateline Long Island, 1964. 27 min. Newsday video on post-war growth. SCLS; 16 mm., SUNY-SB.

Day in the Life of a Revolutionary Soldier, 1986. 26 min. LIVP. LISI, SCLS.

Day in the Life of Colonial Long Island: At the Tavern, 1988. 20 min. LIVP. LISI, SCLS.

deKooning on deKooning, 1982. 16 mm., 58 min. Interview with artist and wife; shows deKooning working in East Hampton Studio. Direct Cinema. HU, SUNY-SB.

Discovery on Long Island, 1964. 28 min. Sponsored by Security National Bank.

Echoes from Long Island's Past, 1873. 16 mm., 20 min. Arts and crafts festival at Stony Brook Museums. NLS, SUNY-SB; video in LILCO, SCLS.

Father Island, Mother Bay, 1972. 16 mm., 20 min. Ecology of marshes and wetlands. NLS; video in LILCO.

Fire Island Ghost Stories, 1988. 21 min. LIVP. LISI, SCHS.

Fowl is Fare, 1966. 16 mm., 9 min. The Long Island duck industry. SUNY-SB.

From Stone, 1987. 16 mm., 29 min. Life and work of sculptor, Jacob Lipkin (North Babylon). SUNY-SB.

Gardiner's Island, 1979. 16 mm., 28 min. Fenwick Productions. SUNY-SB; video in SCLS.

George Dumpson's Place, 1968. 16 mm., 8 min. Portrait of black man and his home in Wantagh. NLS.

Grey Gardens, 1976. 16 mm., 94 min. Edith Bouvier Beale and little Edie at home in East Hampton. NLS.

History of Hauppauge, 1985. 55 min. Lecture and slide by local historian Jack Marr. SCLS.

How Sound is Long Island Sound? 1989, 59 min. GPN (PO Box 80669, Lincoln, NE 68501; 402-472-2087, 800-228-4630). LISI.

How to Produce Video Portraits, 1990. 22 min. Pikes Peak Library District (PO Box 25129, Colorado Springs, CO 80936). How oral history interviews can be combined with historical documents for videotaped community histories. LISI.

Hurricane of '38, The, 1993. 60 min. PBS: American Experience. LISI.

If You Knew Sousa, 1992. 80 min. Bandmaster and composer John Philip Sousa lived in Port Washington, though there are no local references in video. PBS: American Experience series. LISI.

Indian Myths and Legends, 1988. 26 min. LIVP. LISI, SCLS

Indomitable Teddy Roosevelt, The, 1983. 93 min. Excellent biography of TR's public and private life using archival footage and reenactments. Churchill Films (also in 16 mm.). HU, NLS.

Interpreting History through Pictorial Documents, Nancy I. Malen, 1982. 30 min. AASLH. LISI.

Interpreting the Humanities through Museum Exhibits, Fred Schroeder, 1982. 30 min. AASLH. LISI.

It Happened on Long Island, 1974. 16 mm., 28 min. Paintings, poems, and songs depict Long Island's history. NLS, SUNY-SB; video in SCLS.

Jones Beach: An American Riviera, forthcoming one hour documentary by POZ Productions.

Learning History with Artifacts, Barbara G. Carson, 1984. 13 min. AASLH. LISI.

Life of Art, 1986. 16 mm., 20 min. Portrays hitchhikers in 1930s on North Fork; shows farm landscapes. SUNY-SB; video in SCLS.

Lindbergh, 1990. 58 min. PBS: American Experience series. LISI.

Long Island at the Crossroads, 1979. 16 mm., 30 min. Review and discussion of problems facing Long Island; based on *Newsday* series. NLS, SUNY-SB; video in SCLS.

Long Island, The Cradle of Aviation, c. 1970. 16 mm., 22 min. NLS; video in SCLS, LILCO.

Long Island: The Good Life, 1986. 10 min. Produced by the Suffolk County Office of Economic Development. LISI, NLS, SCLS.

Long Island . . . The Suburban Metropolis, 1973. 16 mm., 15 min. Focus on industrial, commercial, residential, and tourism aspects. Long

Island Association of Commerce and Industry. SUNY-SB; video in
  SCHS.
Long Island, U.S.A., 1972. 16 mm., 31 min. Avon documentary on
  pollution, planing, housing issues. NLS
Memorial Day, 1984. 16 mm., 14 min. Memorial Day activities, East
  Hampton. Direct Cinema. SUNY-SB.
Montauk, 1964. 16 mm., 15 min. Contemporary Films. SUNY-SB.
Museum Education: A Tool of Interpretation, by David Estabrook, 1982.
  30 min. AASLH. LISI.
My Father the President, 1981. 23 min. A personal family portrait of
  Theodore Roosevelt, narrated by Ethel Roosevelt Derby. Pyramid
  Films. LISI. Also 16 mm., NLS.
Nassau County's Water Cycle and *Let's Start Saving Water*, 1989. Nassau
  County Department of Public Works.
Naturalists Series: Theodore Roosevelt, 1977. 16 mm., 28 min. TR's
  concern for conservation. Indiana University.
No Home on the Island, 1986. 16 mm., 29 min. Plight of the homeless.
  Video in SCLS.
Nor'Easter, 92: Storm Damage, Nassau County, 1993 News 12. NLS.
Nor'Easter, 92: Storm Damage, Suffolk County, 1993 News 12. NLS.
Once There was a Strike in Levittown, 1979. 60 min. WNET: Bill Moyers'
  Journal series.
The Other Side. 16 mm., 15 min. Wealthy and impoverished in Nassau
  County. OEO. NLS.
Painting from Nature, 1974. 16 mm., 13 min. Dennis Puleston, author
  and illustrator of *A Nature Journal* (1992), describes method of
  painting Long Island birds. Acorn Films. SUNY-SB.
Papa Joe, 1973. 16 mm., 27 min. Study of Joseph Margiotta ("Papa Joe"),
  Nassau County Republican boss (filmed before imprisonment
  and fall from power). NLS, SUNY-SB.
Pathways to the Past, 1984. 18 min. Sources for researching local history;
  written and narrated by Oscar Brand. Bryant Library. HU, LISI,
  NLS.
Patterns of Homespun, 1991. 29 min. NYSHA. Depicts farm life of 1830s.
  LISI.
Pine Barrens, The: Long Island's Wilderness, 1980. 16 mm., 22 min. NLS
  and SUNY-SB; video in LILCO and SCLS (as *Long Island's
  Wilderness . . . The Pine Barrens*).
Present Meets Past: Making History and The Mysteries of Town History,
  1989. 27 min. NYSHA. Designed for students studying local
  history. LISI.
Reeves Park, 1985. 16 mm., 10 min. Community near Riverhead.
  SUNY-SB.
Revolutionary Spies: The Culper Ring, 1987. 21 min. Filmed at Raynham
  Hall. LIVP. LISI, SCLS.
Roy Lichtenstein, 1976. 52 min. Artist working in Long Island studio.
  Blackwood Productions.
Sagamore Hill—National Shrine, 1960. 16 mm., 4 min. Pathe News,
  Milestones of the Century Series. NLS.

Save Our Bays, 1991. 30 min. Produced by Save the Peconic Bays (PO Box 449, Mattituck, NY 11952; 298-4620); accompanying booklet. LISI.

School in Time and Place, A, 1990. 16 min. Cold Spring Harbor School District (75 Goose Hill Rd., Cold Spring Harbor, NY 11724); 692-8036. LISI.

Seasons at Westbury Gardens, The, c. 1970. 16 mm., 18 min. NLS.

Seventy-fifth Anniversary, 1974. 16 mm., 5 min. County Executive Ralph Caso on growth of Nassau. NLS.

Shared Ground, 1990. 19 min. Mudfog Films (PO Box 699, East Moriches, NY 11940; 516-878-4154). Shinnecock oystering project in Southampton. LISI.

Shinnecock: Story of a People, 1976. 16 mm., 20 min. Phoenix. SUNY-SB; video in SCLS.

Song of Myself, 1975. 31 min. Docudrama on Walt Whitman featuring Rip Torn. American Parade series. Phoenix (also 16 mm.). HU.

Teddy Roosevelt—The Right Man at the Right Time, 1974. 28 min. Learning Corporation.

Theodore Roosevelt, American, 1958. 27 min. National Audiovisual Center.

Theodore Roosevelt's Sagamore Hill, 1976. 16 mm., 23 min. Narrated by E. G. Marshall. Also available in video. Aims. NLS.

They Called the Island Long, 1966. 16 mm., 22 min. NLS, SUNY-SB; video in SCLS.

This is Oyster Bay, 1993. 30 min. Town of Oyster Bay Public Information Office.

This Old Town, 1993-1994. Allen Oren's News 12 features on various communities in Nassau and Suffolk counties; each segment is 2-3 min. Four tapes in NLS. An anthology of programs is planned.

Tides of Long Island, 1978. 16 mm., 20 min. NLS; video in SCLS, LILCO.

TR and His Times, 1984. 58 min. PBS: "A Walk Through the 20th Century" series with Bill Moyers. LISI.

Vigilance to Keep, A, 1973. 16 mm., 16 min. Apollo. Environment in Nassau County. NLS.

Walt Whitman, 1988. 60 min. Focus is on poetry and sources. PBS: Voices and Visions series. HU.

Walt Whitman, 1972. 20 min. AIMS Media.

Walt Whitman. 12 min. Films for the Humanities and Science.

Walt Whitman, Endlessly Rocking, 1986. 21 min. A humorous contemporary approach to poetry; designed for ages 14-17. Barr Films.

Walt Whitman: Poet for a New Age, 1971. 29 min. Encyclopedia Britannica. 16 mm. SUNY-SB. Also available in video.

Walt Whitman, Sweet Bird of Freedom, 1991. 29 min. Barr Films.

Walt Whitman: The Good Gray Poet, 1985. 14 min. Southwest Queens Educational Television (Community School Dist. #27; available at Walt Whitman Birthplace, Huntington Station, 427-5240). LISI.

Walt Whitman's Civil War, 1969. 16 mm., 23 min. SUNY-SB.

Walt Whitman's Civil War, 1972. 15 min. Churchill Films.

Walt Whitman's Leaves of Grass, 1965. 16 mm., 20 min. SUNY-SB.

Walt Whitman's Western Journey, 1965. 16 mm., 15 min. SUNY-SB.

Water: Long Island's Most Precious Resource, 1991. 19 min. Long Island Water Conference (575 Broad Hollow Road, Melville, NY 11747-5076; 516-756-8000 x410). LISI.

Whaling Saga: The Martha Tunstall Smith Story, 1986. 21 min. Filmed at Sag Harbor Whaling Museum. LIVP. LISI, SCLS.

What Harvest for the Reaper, 1968. 16 mm., 59 min. Migrant farm workers (Cutchogue). NET/Indiana University. SUNY-SB.

William Merritt Chase: Summers at Shinnecock, 1987. 26 min. National Gallery of Art (2000B South Club Drive, Landover, MD 20785). LISI.

World of Tomorrow, The: The 1939 World's Fair, 1986. 82 min. PBS. HU, NLS.

World That [Robert] Moses Built, The, 1988. 58 min. PBS: American Experience. LISI.

Yesterday's Time, 1898-1940: A Recollection of Bygone Queens Neighborhoods, 1989. 24 min. History Films, Inc. (Richard Altomonte, 1846 Fairhaven Rd., East Meadow, NY 11554; 516-351-9620). LISI.

Part II: Additional Audio-Visual Resources in LISI

Videos

Archi Awards, 1990. 28 min. American Institute of Architects (AIA), Long Island Chapter. The AIA has designated LISI as respository for its annual architecture (Archi) awards and LISI also has, for example, photographs and slides of AIA's 1992 and 1993 awards.

Back to Port [Washington], 1994. 25 min. Cablevision documentary on community's history.

Baymen, The, 1994. 90 min. Cablevision "Special Editions" documentary on East End baymen.

Biological Revolution: 100 Years of Science at Cold Spring Harbor, 1988. 30 min. Cold Spring Harbor Laboratory.

Building Bridges Between School and Community, 1993. 15 mins. McKissick Museum. Junior high school students in Georgetown, SC interview family and residents for local history. LISI.

Building the American Dream: Levittown, N.Y., 1994. 60 min. HU and Cablevision. LISI.

Christopher Morley's Long Island by Long Island's Christopher Morley, 1990; 70 min. Readings from Morley's writings about Long Island.

Critical Choices Convention, NYS Bicentennial of the Constitution, 1988. 30 min.

Discover Your Long Island Heritage, 1987. 24 min. Nassau County Museum. Introduction to museums and preserves in the county system. A slide/tape program converted to video by HU's TV Institute.

Echoes on the Sound, 1985. 27 min. Folklife. Sands Point history, written and narrated by Oscar Brand.

Englishman's Fantasy, An: The Estate of William Robertson Coe, 1986. 35 min. Slide presentation by Lorraine Gilligan at LISI Conference.

Evolution of Agriculture on Long Island, 1992. 60 min. Cablevision "Special Educations." Focuses on a number of farm families in Suffolk throughout one year. LISI.

F. Scott Fitzgerald Conference, HU, 1992. Presentations by Joann P. Krieg, Robert Sargent, Judith Spinzia, Raymond Spinzia, and Roger Wunderlich on "Fitzgerald and Long Island" and "Long Island's North Shore Gold Coast Era: Setting for Great Gatsby."

George Washington's Tour of Long Island, 1790, c. 1976. 7 min. Newsday news feature.

Hallockville Museum Farm, 1986. 13 min. Introduction to museum.

Life and Times of John Lewis Childs, 1991. 31 min. Floral Park Women's Club. Childs was the founder of Floral Park.

LIRR: A Reflection, 1984. 13 min. Long Island Rail Road commemorates 150th anniversary; includes archival footage.

Long Island State Park Commission, documentary footage on New York and Long Island parks and parkways, including Jones Beach; 1930s and early 1940s. 7 hours.

Long Island 1776: The Way it Was, 1976. 26 min. Reenactment by Huntington Militia of Long Island's reaction to the Declaration of Independence. Newsday.

Long Island [Vanderbilt] Motor Parkway and its Garden City Toll Lodge, 1993. 20 min. Toll Lodge Preservation Association.

Local History as Universal History, 1986. 60 min. Opening and keynote address (slide presentation) by Thomas J. Schlereth at LISI conference.

Maritime Traditions of the South Shore, 1988. 28 min. Freeport Arts Council. A slide/tape presentation by folklorist Nancy Solomon; converted to video by HU's TV Institute.

Native Americans of Montauk. Ten tapes from two-day symposium at Guild Hall, 1991.

Newsday: 50th Anniversary, 1992. 15 min. Overview of *Newsday's* and Long Island's history since 1940s.

On Doing Local History, 1987. 50 min. Talk by Carol Kammen at SUNY, Brockport.

Our Long Island Heritage, 1975. 5 minutes each. Historian Myron Luke describes six historic sites and museums (Conklin House, Saddle Rock Grist Mill, Sands-Willets House, Rock Hall, St. George's Episcopal Church Hempstead, and Raynham Hall). Mini-documentaries on WLIW, Channel 21.

Our Town, 1987. 48 min. Storyteller Heather Forest gives an overview of local history. Plainview-Old Bethpage School District.

Presentation Days, 1987, 30 min. Bridgehampton School 7th and 8th grade students present work on local cultural heritage.

Project 2000: Culture, News 12. Brief news report on "white paper"; interview with Joann Krieg.

Roslyn Portrait, 1990. 5 min. History Film Inc. Also *Interviews*, archival footage of interviews with Roy Moger, Roslyn Village Historian (40 min.) and Ray Jacobs (20 min.), 1990. History Films, Inc.

Sampler, 1988. 70 min. Clips from ten videotapes on Long Island
history in the LISI collections.
Society for the Preservation of Long Island Antiquities (SPLIA),
orientation films: *The Thompson House*, 6 min; *Joseph Lloyd Manor
House* (1986), 10 min; *Long Island Slavery: Six Portraits* (1991), 12
min, slaves at the Lloyd Manor House.
Suburban Town Meeting, 1987. 13 min. Session from LISI Suburbia
Re-examined Conference.
Syosset Story: 1900-1950, 1992. 55 min. Syosset Public Library. Focuses
on 1920s-1940s.
Teacher's Room: A History of the Levittown Schools, 1947-1987, 1987. 30
min. HU School of Education and Levittown Teacher Center.
Teedie, 1989. 25 min. Coe Films. Focuses on the childhood of Theodore
Roosevelt.
Three Centuries of Growth: Nassau County and its Courthouse, 1991. 8 min.
Nassau County Museum.
Through the Eyes of Hal Fullerton, 1994. 32 min. Cablevision
documentary on turn-of-century special agent and photographer
for LIRR. See also Charles Sachs, *Blessed Isle: Hal B. Fullerton and
His Image of Long Island, 1897-1927*, 1991 LISI publication.
Typical Architecture and Timeless Shrine: The Walt Whitman Birthplace,
1987. 12 min. Slide presentation by Marilyn Oser at the May 1986
LISI Conference later videotaped at HU's TV Institute.
Viacom Visits . . . Hauppauge, 1987. 12 min. Historical overview by
Suffolk historian J. Lance Mallamo, 12 min. Also *Viacom Visits . . .
Port Jefferson*, 28 min.; *Viacom Visits . . . Sayville*, 27 min.; *Viacom
Visits Stony Brook*, 19 min. (includes interview with Mrs. Ward
Melville), 19 min.
Video Views of Long Island People & Places, Past & Present, 1990. 50 mins.
Clips from seven videos prepared for LISI conference.
Video Views on Long Island Studies, 1991. 38 min. Clips from eight
videos, prepared for LISI conference.
The Way We Were, c. 1986. Plainview-Old Bethpage School District.
Local history.
Yorkers, The, 1990. 20 min. NYSHA. History clubs for grades 4-12.

Audiotapes and Slide-Tape Programs

Crabgrass Frontier: Suburbanization and the New York Experience, The,
1985. Audiotape of address by Kenneth Jackson at LISI-New York
State History Conference.
Fairfield Porter: An American Intimist, 1988. Parrish Art Museum.
Slide-cassette program. (Can be borrowed from Parrish.)
Genealogical Workshops, Suffolk County Historical Society. Various
historical and genealogical topics.
Indians of Lenapehoking. Slide-tape program by Herbert Kraft.
Long Island State, The, 1984. The Old Bethpage Singers perform
patriotic, comic, sentimental, and descriptive songs of nineteenth
century America. Cassette.

Long Island Studies Council meetings, 1986-date. Variety of speakers
   and topics.
LISI. Most LISI conference and symposium presentations are on
   audiotape including Suburbia Re-Examined, 1987; Robert Moses,
   1988; Building Long Island/Architecture, 1989; Theodore
   Roosevelt, 1990; Exploring African-American History, 1991;
   Maritime Heritage, 1992; Hempstead, 1993; Women and the Sea,
   1995, and one-day symposia, 1987-date (a few of the slide
   presentations are on videotape); a complete list of speakers and
   titles is available at LISI.
People of the Sea, Suffolk maritime traditions; slide-cassette program.
Theodore Roosevelt: Long Island's Most Famous American, 1986.
   Audiotape of LISI talk by Michael D'Innocenzo.
Using Archives in the Classroom, 1990. Audiotape of LISI Archives Week
   presentation by Noel Gish.
Walt Whitman Here in Trimming Square, 1992. Symposium at Adelphi
   University; audiotape of presentations by Thomas Heffernan,
   Joann Krieg, Harrison Hunt, Natalie Naylor, and Paul van Wie.
William Merritt Chase: Portrait of an American Artist, 1987. Parrish Art
   Museum. Slide-tape program. (Can be borrowed from Parrish.)

Resources and Guides for Local History

Most of these titles are recommended for teachers and other adults; those designed for younger students have grade level indicated. The New York State Historical Association (NYSHA) has developed excellent resources for local and New York State history, focusing on grades 4 and 7–8. It sponsors Yorker and Young Yorker clubs in schools throughout the state and week-long Seminars in American Culture in July for teachers, museum personnel, and others interested in history and artifacts. Membership benefits include subscriptions to *New York History* and *New York Heritage.* NYSHA's Fenimore Book Store is an excellent source of educational materials and a catalog is available. Contact: New York State Historical Association, P.O. Box 800, Cooperstown, NY 13326; 607-547-2533.

The American Association for State and Local History (AASLH) has published many books and leaflets useful to teachers, historical societies, and others interested in local history. Information: AASLH, 530 Church Street, Suite 600, Nashville, TN 37219; 615-255-2971, fax 615-255-2979.

The Museum Education Department of Old Sturbridge Village has produced many books and other resources for teachers; although focused on New England, they can be adapted for other areas. Some titles are listed below. Contact: Mail Order Department, Museum Gift Shop, Old Sturbridge Village, Sturbridge, MA 01566.

Many of the materials listed here are available in the Hofstra University Libraries, either in the Long Island Studies Institute (LISI) in the Library Services Center on the West Campus or the Curriculum Materials Center (CMC) on the ground floor, Axinn Library. SCHS indicates title is available at the Weathervane Shop, Suffolk County Historical Society, 300 W. Main St., Riverhead 11901 (727-2881); OBVR designates the museum shop at Old Bethpage Village Restoration.

Abhau, Marcy, ed. *Architecture in Education: A Resource of Imaginative Ideas and Tested Activities.* Philadelphia: Foundation for Architecture, 1986. Grades K-12; NYSHA.

AASLH Technical Leaflets. Topics include "Cemetery Transcribing"; "Tape-Recording Local History"; "History for Young People: Projects and Activities"; "Producing a Slide-Tape Show"; and "Historic Houses as Learning Laboratories." Available in LISI.

Aibel-Weiss, Wendy. *Today's Children in Yesterday's Houses.* Setauket: Society for the Presrvation of Long Island Antiquities, 1986. Written for museum professionals, but of interest to teachers for ideas on using objects in studying history. SCHS.

Baum, Willa K. *Oral History for the Local Historical Society,* 3d. ed. AASLH, 1987.

Butchart, Ronald E. *Local Schools: Exploring their History.* AASLH, 1986.

Cobblestone. Monthly history magazine for children. Back issues on "America's Lighthouses," 2 (June 1981), 6 (no. 681), "Seafaring Life," 9 (April 1988), 4 (no. 488), and "Whaling in America," 5 (April 1984), 4 (no. 484),"Genealogy" (no. 1180). Available ($3.95 each) from Cobblestone, 20 Grove St., Peterborough, NH 03458. Grades 4-7.

Crawford, Joyce and Jo Ann Secor. *Once Upon an Island: An Activity-Based Guide to Teaching Local History.* Staten Island: Staten Island Children's Museum, 1983. Geared to fourth grade; can be adapted for Long Island.

D'Alelio, Jane. *I Know That Building! Discovering Architecture with Activities and Games.* Washington, DC: Preservation Press, 1989. Grades 4-9; OBVR.

Danzer, Gerald A. *Public Places: Exploring their History.* AASLH, 1987.

Felt, Thomas E. *Researching, Writing and Publishing Local History.* AASLH, 1981.

Gardner, James B. and George Rollie Adams, eds. *Ordinary People and Everyday Life: Perspectives on the New Social History.* AASLH, 1983.

Genealogy. Boy Scout Merit Badge pamphlet. Available in libraries and Boy Scout supply stores.

History News. Monthly magazine of AASLH.

Hoomes, Eleanor. *At the Grass Roots Level: A Community Research and Writing Project.* Hawthorne, NJ: Educational Impressions, 1988. Grades 7-12. CMC.

Houts, Mary D. "How to be a History Dectective." Designed by the Hershey Museum for high school students to use census, newspaper, and other records. Hershey Museum, 170 West Hershey Park Drive, Hershey, PA 17033-2729 (717-535-3439). Copy in CMC.

Howe, Barbara et al. *Houses and Homes: Exploring Their History.* AASLH, 1983.

Jolly, Brad. *Videotaping Local History.* AASLH, 1982.

Kalman, Bobbie, ed. Early Settler Life Series. Fifteen titles, e.g. *Early Artisans, Early Schools.* New York: Crabtree Publishing, 1980s. Illustrated paperbacks; grades 3-5. OBVR, NYSHA.

Kammen, Carol. *On Doing Local History.* AASLH, 1986.

———. *Plain as a Pipestem: Essays on Local History.* Interlaken, NY: Heart of the Lakes, 1989.

Kerr, K. Austin. *Local Businesses: Exploring Their History.* AASLH, 1990.

Kyvig, David and Myron A. Marty. *Nearby History: Exploring the Past Around You.* AASLH, 1982.

Mahoney, James. *Local History: A Guide for Research and Writing.* Washington, DC: National Education Association, 1981. CMC.

Metcalf, Fay and Matthew Cowney. *Using Local History in the Classroom*. AASLH, 1981.

Neville, Emily C. and Marianna Pluchino Stout. *A Look at Our Town: Village, City, County Government*, 1982. New York State Education Department and League of Women Voters. Section 1 for teachers and section 2 for fourth grade students.

New York State Historical Association. *Present Meets Past*, 1989. Videotape (26 min.) and teacher's manual on the study of history. Topics include family, home, school, work, neighborhoods, landscape, and architecture. Grade 4. Videotape and teacher's manual, $69; see also books by Gretchen Sorin listed below. Video in LISI.

———. "Field Workbook Leaflets for Fourth Grade for Local History." Collected reprints; $8 for each set of 7–8 topics with student and teacher editions. Issued monthly during school year; subscriptions available. Copies in LISI and CMC.

New York State Museum. *Tracking Down the Past*, 1983. Teaching kit with photographs, artifacts, documents, oral history tapes, and student booklets. Grades 4+. Contact the Museum, 60 Commerce Ave., Albany, NY 12296.

Newhouse, Mark. *Using the Newspaper to Rediscover New York*. Newsday, 1992. CMC.

Old Sturbridge Village. Packets of documents ("Childhood," "Youth," "The Farm Family") and activities ("Kitchen Crafts," "Fun and Games"), and books of activities with notes for teachers (*Community: People and Places* and *Family: Past and Present*, 1985), grades 4–8.

———. *The Small Town Sourcebook: Reliving New England's Past through Pictures, Ads, and Personal Histories*, 2 vols., 1979. Teacher's Guide; grades 4–12.

Pathways to the Past. Videotape (18 mins.) on researching local history, narrated by Oscar Brand, with a Teacher's Manual by Glenn M. Pribeck, 1983. Produced by and available from the Bryant Library, Paper Mill Rd, Roslyn; 621-2240. Copy in LISI.

Pierce, Susan. *Street Sleuths! Learning to Look at Buildings*. Huntington: Huntington Historical Society, 1987.

Pikes Peak Library District. *How to Produce Video Portraits*. A video guide to enhancing videotaped oral history interviews with local history; 22 min. (PO Box 1579, Colorado Springs, CO 80901; 719-531-6333). Copy in LISI.

Provenzo, Eugene F. and A. B. Provenzo. *Pursuing the Past*. Menlo Park, CA: Addison-Wesley, 1984. Textbook with teacher's guide. Good suggestions on using oral history, photos, cemeteries, and family history. Grade 7+ (can be adapted for grade 4). Copy in CMC.

Researching the History of Your School: Suggestions for Students and Teachers. Albany: New York State Archives, 1985.

Roe, Kathleen. *Teaching with Historical Records*. Albany: New York State Archives, 1981. Copy in CMC.

Russo, David J. *Families and Communities: A New View of American History.* AASLH, 1974.
Schlereth, Thomas J. *Artifacts and the American Past.* AASLH, 1980.
———. ed. *Material Culture: A Research Guide.* Lawrence: University Press of Kansas, 1985.
———. *Material Culture Studies in America.* AASLH, 1982.
———. *Cultural History and Material Culture: Everyday Life, Landscapes, Museums.* Charlottesville: University Press of Virginia, 1990.
Sorin, Gretchen. *Present Meets Past: A Guide to Exploring Community History.* Vol. 1: *All About Me;* vol. 2: *The Place Where I Live,* NYSHA, 1987, 1988. Includes teacher's guide and student activity sheets utilizing primary documents, photographs, paintings, and prints. Grade 4, 92 pp. each. Copies in CMC and LISI.
Szekely, George and Dianna Gabay. *A Study of a Community: Staten Island Architecture and Environment.* New York: Staten Island Continum of Education, 1980. Curriculum guide for teachers on the built environment; adaptable.
Weitzman, David. *My Backyard History Book.* Boston: Little Brown and Co., 1975. Grades 4-10; SCHS.
———. *Underfoot: An Everyday Guide to Exploring the American Past.* New York: Charles Scribner's Sons, 1976.
Wind, James P., *Places of Worship: Exploring Their History.* AASLH, 1990.

Long Island's Native American Indians

Natalie A. Naylor

Probable Meaning of Indian Place Names

One of the legacies from the Native Americans on Long Island are place names. In fact, the names traditionally used to identify the Indian groups are descriptions of the land where they lived. The meaning of those names, however, is not clear. There were linguistic differences between the "Lenni Lenape speakers of western Long Island and the Southern New England language-variant speakers of eastern Long Island" and a cultural boundary, between East River and Orient cultures at approximately the present-day Nassau Suffolk boundary. It is uncertain, however, if this coincided with the linguistic boundary, which may have been further west (Gaynell Stone, "Long Island as America: A New Look at the First Inhabitants," *Long Island Forum*, 1 [Spring 1989]: 163).

Thomas Jefferson and John Lyon Gardiner collected some Indian words in the 1790s when there were only a few native speakers. William Wallace Tooker, working in the late nineteenth and early twentieth century, did extensive research to determine the "probable signification" of Algonquian place names. He was unable to rely on native-speaking informants, since the languages were virtually extinct. Nancy Bonvillain has indicated that Tooker's definitions are of "questionable linguistic accuracy" (in *Languages and Lore of the Long Island Indians*, ed. Gaynell Stone Levine and Nancy Bonvillain, p. 13).

Robert Steven Grumet, a cultural anthropologist, compiled information on place names in New York City including western Long Island (Brooklyn and Queens). Grumet relies heavily on Tooker and other "amateur enthusiasts," since he believes "no study of the cultural and historical significance of the Native American place names . . . can be complete without them" (*Native American Place Names in New York City*, 1981).

Following are traditional name definitions from Tooker's, *Indian Place Names on Long Island*, 1911 (reprinted, 1962). Tooker has nearly 500 Indian names and many more varient spellings in his book.

Amagansett—well, well plain, or well hollow.
Aquebogue (Ucque-baug)—the end of the water-place or head of the bay.
Canarsie—fenced place.
Cantiaque (Cantiagge)—where trees are being blazed.
Caumsett—at, about, or in the neighborhood of a sharp rock.
Comac (Comack, Winne-Commack— a house, a place, a field; good land, pleasant field, fine country.
Gowanus—the sleeper, he rests.
Hauppauge—flooded, overflowed land.
Jamaica (Yemacah)—beaver.
Manhansett (Manhansack-Ahaquatuwamock; Shelter Island)— island land or neighborhood.
Manhattan (Manahatin)—the hill island.
Massapeague (Marsapeague, Massapequa)—great water land, land on the great cove.
Mastic—great river.
Matinnecock—high land, at the place to look around from.
Mattanwake (Matowa)—Long Island.
Mattituck—place without wood, destitute of trees.
Meitowax (name for Long Island)—land of the periwinkle, country of the ear-shell.
Merrick (Merriack— at the barren land, a plain.
Montauk (Meuntacut)—fortified town.
Nassakeag (Mesakaks)—sachem of the Nissequogues.
Noyack—point or corner of land.
Patchogue (Pochoug)—a turning place (of river); name of Indian.
Paumanack (Pommanock; name of Eastern Long Island)— land of tribute.
Peconic (Peaconeck)—a small plantation.
Poosepatuck (Pusspa'tuck)—union of two rivers and a fall into tide water, where a cove or creek bursts forth.
Quogue (shortened form of Quaquanantuck)—cove or estuary where it [the meadow] quakes or trembles.
Rockaway (Rechouwhacky)—sandy place, lonely place.
Ronkonkoma (Raconkumake)—the fence or boundary fishing-place.
Sagamore—chief or sachem.
Sagaponack—place where big ground nuts grow.
Seawanhacky (Sewanhaka; name for Long Island)—island of shells, sewan [wampum] country.
Secatogue (Secoutagh)—black or dark colored land.
Setauket (Seatauke)—land at the river, or land at the mouth of a river or creek.

Shinnecock (Shinnekuke)— at the level land or country.
Unkechaug—land or place beyond the hill.
Wantagh (Wiandance)—see Wyandance.
Wyandance (sachem of Paumanack)—the wise speaker or
    talker.
Yaphank—bank of a river.

Bibliography

Many books, especially most of the older works (including some still in print), perpetuate myths about "thirteen tribes" and do not reflect current scholarship. Even recent publications may err. Some of the older books, however, still do have useful information. Some of these titles deal with Northeast Woodland Indians (Delaware, Lenape, or New England Indians) rather than specifically Long Island; the information on culture is similar.

Grade level is indicated for books suitable for younger readers; some can be used with younger ages with adult guidance. Abbreviations: LISI indicates the Long Island Studies Institute; *LIHJ, Long Island Historical Journal;* OBVR, Old Bethpage Village Restoration (museum shop); SCAA, the Suffolk County Archaeological Society; SCHS, the Suffolk County Historical Society (Weathervane Shop); and VF, Vertical File at LISI. Addresses for organizations are at the end of this section under "Museums, Organizations, and Sources."

Bailey, Paul. *The Thirteen Tribes on Long Island,* 1959. Rev. ed. Syosset: Friends for Long Island's Heritage, 1982. 25 pp. Gr 7 +. OBVR.
Barnes, Gean Finch. *Tales of the High Hills: Legends of the Montauk Indians,* ed. Margaret H. Lamb. East Hampton: Town of East Hampton, 1975.
Brooklyn Historical Society. *New World Encounters; Jasper Danckaert's View of Indian Life in 17th Century Brooklyn,* 1986. Exhibit catalog. LISI-VF.
Cerrato, Robert M., Heather V. E. Wallace, and Kent G. Lightfoot. "Tidal and Seasonal Patterns in the Chondrophore of the Soft-Shell Clam *Mya arenaria.*" *Biol. Bull.* 181 (1991): 307-11. LISI-VF.
Coles, Robert R. *The Long Island Indian.* Glen Cove: Little Museum, 1954. 58 pp.
Conkey, Laura E, Ethel Boissevain, and Ives Goddard. "Indians of Southern New England and Long Island: Late Period." In *Handbook of North American Indians,* ed. William C. Sturtevant, 15: 177-89. Washington, DC: Smithsonian, 1978. Also in the *Hand-*

---

* In print, 1994.

book, see: Dean Snow, "Late Prehistory of the East Coast"; Ives Goddard, "Eastern Algonquian Languages"; T. J. Brasser, "Early Indian-European Contacts," and Salwan's essay cited below.

Cuffee, Nathan J. and Lydia Jocelyn. *Lords of the Soil,* 1905. Reprinted; Southampton: Yankee Peddler Book Co., 1974. Historical novel, co-authored by a Montauk; a "romantic blend of folklore, history, and myth" (John Strong, review in *LIHJ,* 3 [1991]: 256).

Denver Art Museum Indian Leaflets, 1931-1932 (reprinted, c. 1972, but now out of print; each 4 pp., gr. 7+): no. 31 *Iroquoian and Algonkin Wampum;* no. 49 *Long Island Indian Tribes;* no. 50 *Long Island Indian Culture.*

Dyson, Verne. *Heather Flower and Other Indian Tales of Long Island.* Port Washington: Ira J. Friedman, 1967. Gr. 8.

Gehring, Charles T. and Robert S. Grumet. "Observations of the Indians from Jasper Danckaert's Journal, 1679-1680." *The William and Mary Quarterly,* 3d Series, 44 (January 1987): 104-20. Journal in college libraries; article in LISI-VF.

Golder, William E. *Long Island's First Inhabitants.* 2d ed. Southold Indian Museum, 1988. Gr. 10+. See critical review in *LIHJ* [Fall 1990]: 144-6.

Gonzalez, Ellice. "Tri-racial Isolates in a Bi-racial Society: Poosepatuck Ambiguity and Conflict." In *Strategies for Survival: American Indians in the Eastern United States,* ed. Frank W. Porter. Westport, CT: Greenwood Press, 1986.

Gottlieb, William. *History of Sachem Tackapausha and Long Island Indians in Colonial North Hempstead.* North Hempstead Town, 1977. 53 pp.

Grumet, Robert S. *The Lenape.* New York: Chelsea House, 1989. Listed as "juvenile," but the vocabulary is at least at 8th grade reading level; good photographs.

_____. *Native American Place Names in New York City.* New York: Museum of the City of New York, 1981. Includes some of eastern Long Island as well as Brooklyn and Queens.

Halsey, Carolyn D. *The Indians of Long Island,* 1986. 24 pp. Gr. 3-6. $3.50. SCHS

Hawk, William. "The Revitalization of the Matinecock Indian Tribe of New York." Ph.D. dissertation, University of Wisconsin, 1964. Copy in LISI.

Hunter, Lois Marie. *The Shinnecock Indians.* Privately printed, 1950. 90 pp.

Irwin, R. Stephen. *Hunters of the Eastern Forest.* Blaine, WA: Hancock, 1984. 52 pp. SCHS.

Jameson, J. Franklin. *Narratives of New Netherland.* New York: Barnes and Noble, 1909. First-hand ethographic information in accounts by Juet, DeLaet, Van Wessenaer, and DeVries, 11-60, 207-34.

Jarey, Cornell, ed. *Historic Chronicles of New Amsterdam, Colonial New York and Early Long Island.* New York: Ira Friedman, 1968. Includes ethnographic information from Charles Wooley, *Two Years Journal in New York, 1678-1680* (1: 16-54) and Daniel Denton, *Brief Description of New York* (1670; 2: 6-13).

Kalin, Robert J., Kent G. Lightfoot, and James Moore. "Soil Patterns and Prehistoric Sites in Suffolk County, New York." *Man in the Northeast* 36 (1988): 1-20.

Kaplan, Daniel H. *A Bibliography on the Archaeology and Ethnography of Coastal New York.* Port Washington, NY, 1982. Available free from Nassau County Museum/Sands Point Preserve, 95 Middleneck Road, Port Washington 11050.

Kraft, Herbert C. *The Lenape: Archaeology, History and Ethnography.* Newark: New Jersey Historical Society, 1986 (paperback, 1988). Lenape were in New Jersey, eastern Pennsylvania, southeastern New York (including western Long Island), and northern Delaware.

_____. *The Lenape Indians of New Jersey.* South Orange, NJ: Seton Hall University Museum, 1987. 8.5"x11", 64 pp. Gr. 4; $5.

Kraft, Herbert C. and John T. Kraft. *The Indians of Lenapehoking.* South Orange, NJ: Seton Hall University Museum, 1985. 8.5 "x 11", 45 pp. Gr. 9+. Copy in LISI and Hofstra's Curriculum Materials Center, Axinn Library. $5.

Kalin, Robert J., Kent G. Lightfoot, and James Moore. "Soil Patterns and Prehistoric Sites in Suffolk County, New York." *Man in the Northeast* 36 (1988): 1-20.

Lightfoot, Kent G. "Shell Midden Diversity: A Case Example from Coastal New York." *North American Archaeologist* 6, no. 4 (1985): 289-324. LISI-VF.

_____. "Archaeological Investigations of Prehistoric Sites on Eastern Long Island." In *Evoking a Sense of Place,* edited by Joann P. Krieg, pp. 31-43. Interlaken, NY: Heart of the Lakes, 1988. Final reports have not been completed on this site, but LISI-VF has offprints of other articles by Lightfoot on his findings at a Shelter Island site.

_____. "Coastal Archaeology: Ecotones and Drowned Terrestrial Sites." *Coasts, Plains and Deserts,* edited by Sylvia Gaines. *Anthropological Research Papers* (Arizona State University.) 38 (1987): 145-53. LISI-VF.

Lightfoot, Kent G., and Robert M. Cerrato. "Prehistoric Shellfish Exploitation in Coastal New York." *Journal of Field Archaeology* 15 (1988): 141-9. LISI-VF.

_____. "Regional Patterns of Clam Harvesting Along the Atlantic Coast of North America." *Archaeology of Eastern North America* 17 (1989): 31-46. LISI-VF.

Lightfoot, Kent G., Robert M. Cerrato, and Heather V. E. Wallace. "Prehistoric Shellfish-Harvesting Strategies: Implications from the Growth Patterns of Soft-Shell Clams (*Mya arenaria*)." *Antiquity* 67, no. 255 (1993): 358-69. LISI-VF.

Lightfoot, Kent G., Robert Kalin, and James Moore. "Prehistoric Hunter-Gatherers of Shelter Island, New York: An Archaeological Study of the Mashomack Preserve." *Contributions of the University of California Archaeological Research Facility* 46 (1987). LISI-VF.

Lightfoot, Kent G., Robert Kalin, Owen Lindauer, and Linda Wicks. "Coastal New York Settlement Patterns: A Perspective from Shelter Island." *Man in the Northeast* 30 (1985): 59-82. LISI-VF.

118   *Native American Indians*

Lightfoot, Kent G., and James Moore. "Interior Resources Exploitation: A Woodland Settlement Model for Long Island, New York." *Anthropology* 8 (1985): 15-40. LISI-VF.

Mann, H. *A Brief Account of the Indians in the Township of North Hempstead,* 1924. Reprint; Great Neck: Friedman, 1949. 32 pp.

Moeller, Roger W. *Guide to Indian Artifacts of the Northeast.* Blaine, WA: Hancock House/American Indian Archaeological Institute (Washington, CT), 1984. 31 pp. pamphlet.

Morice, John H. "The Indians of Long Island." In *Long Island: A History of Two Great Counties,* ed. Paul Bailey, 1: 107-45. New York: Lewis Publishing, 1949.

Nassau County Museum, *The Indian Archaeology of Long Island.* Leaflet no. 17; 8 pp. Gr. 9+. A good brief overview of Indian culture from Garvies Point Museum.

Overton, Jacqueline. *Indian Life on Long Island: Family, Work, Play, Legends, Heroes,* 1938. Reprint; Port Washington, Ira J. Friedman, 1963. 150 pp. Gr. 4+.

Peña, Elizabeth Shapiro. "Wampum Production in New Netherland and Colonial New York: The Historical and Archaeological Context." Ph.D. thesis, Boston University, 1990. Copy in LISI.

Ritchie, William A. *The Stony Brook Site and Its Relation to Archaic and Transitional Cultures on Long Island.* Albany: New York State Museum, 1959.

___. *The Archaeology of New York State.* Garden City: The Natural History Press, 1969.

Salwen, Bert. "Indians of Southern New England and Long Island: Early Period." In *Handbook of North American Indians,* ed. William C. Sturtevant, 15: 160-76.

Stone, Gaynell. *Long Island Native Americans: Selected Readings,* 1991. SCAA, 214 pp. Limited edition of a college text which reprints useful articles. Copy in LISI.

___. *The Montauk: Native Americans of Eastern Long Island,* 1991. Exhibit leaflet, 8 pp., $3. Gr. 8. SCHS, Garvies Point.

___. "Long Island's America: A New Look at the First Inhabitants," *Long Island Historical Journal* 1 (Spring 1989): 159-69. The best brief introduction to current scholarship. See also her chapter, "Long Island Before the Europeans," in *Between Ocean and Empire: An Illustrated History of Long Island,* ed. Robert B. MacKay et al. (Northridge, CA: Windsor, 1985), 10-29.

Strong, John A. "From Hunter to Servant: Patterns of Accommodation to Colonial Authority in Eastern Long Island Indian Communities," *To Know the Place: Teaching Local History,* edited by Joann P. Krieg, pp. 15-23. Hempstead, NY: Long Island Studies Institute, 1986.

___. See his articles listed in the references to his article "Indian Labor During the Post-Contact Period" earlier in this book (and other references there as well). Also forthcoming book on Long Island Indians.

Suffolk County Archaeological Association (SCAA), *Readings in Long Island Archaeology and Ethnohistory;* scholarly series available from SCAA, SCHS, and OBVR:
1. *Early Papers in Long Island Archaeology,* ed. Gaynell Stone Levine, 1977. 81 pp.
2. **The Coastal Archaeology Reader Selections from the New York State Archaeological Association Bulletin, 1954-1977,* ed. James E. Truex, 1978. 440 pp.
3. **History and Archaeology of the Montauk Indian,* ed. Gaynell Stone Levine, 1979. 218 pp. Revised edition forthcoming.
4. **Languages and Lore of the Long Island Indians,* ed. Gaynell Stone Levine and Nancy Bonvillain, 1980. 320 pp.
5. **The Second Coastal Archaeology Reader,* ed. James E. Truex, 1982. 312 pp.
6. *The Shinnecock Indians: A Culture History,* ed. Gaynell Stone, 1983. 404 pp.
Suggs, Robert C. *The Archaeology of New York.* New York: Crowell, 1966. 156 pp. Gr. 7+.
Tooker, William Wallace. *The Indian Place-Names of Long Island,* 1911. Reprint; Port Washington: Ira J. Friedman, 1962.
Treadwell, Donald E. (Chief Lone Otter). **My People, the Unkechaug: The Story of a Long Island Indian Tribe.* New Amsterdam: Kiva, 1992. SCHS.
Truex, James and Gaynell Stone. **A Way of Life: Indians of Long Island. Prehistoric Period.* Stony Brook: SCAA, [1985]. 14 pp. Gr. 5+. $4.
Tucker, Toba. *A Shinnecock Portrait: Photographs of the Shinnecock Indians on Long Island.* East Hampton: Guild Hall, 1987. Includes essays by John Strong and Madeline Burnside.
Van Der Donck, Adriaen. *A Description of the New Netherlands.* Syracuse: Syracuse University Press, 1968; pp. 71-109 includes ethnographic insights.
Werner, Ben Jr. *The Indians of Long Island, New York and Coastal Connecticut.* Port Jefferson: Privately printed, 1973. 31 pp. Gr. 10+.
Wilbur, C. Keith. **The New England Indians.* Chester, CT: Globe Pequot Press, 1978. 103 pp. Gr. 7+, $10.95 paperback. Very good illustrations and information.
———. **Indian Handcrafts.* Chester, CT: Globe Pequot Press, 1990.
Wyckoff, Edith Hay. *The Fabled Past Tales of Long Island.* Port Washington: I.J. Friedman, 1978, pp. 3-46. Gr. 4+.

Teaching Materials and Resources

Barcel, Ellen N. **Exploring Long Island Archaeology: Southold Indian Museum Teacher's Guide and Resource Kit for Grades 4-6,* 1987.
———. **Exploring Long Island Archaeology: Southold Indian Museum Teacher's Guide and Resource Kit for Grades 7-9,* 1987.
Brundin, Judith, et al. *The Native People of the Northeast Woodlands: An Educational Resource Publication,* 1990. An excellent 240-page curriculum guide for elementary and middle school teachers with background information, many suggestions for activities, and lists

of sources. Published by Museum of the American Indian-Heye
Foundation. Copy in CMC and LISI.
Indian Myths and Legends, c. 1987. 20 minute videotape. Long Island
Video Project, c/o Madonia, 2 Albion Place, E. Patchogue, 11772;
289-0843. Can preview in LISI.
Kraft, Herbert C. 80 color slides on Lenape Indians, 30 min. cassette
tape narration and printed copy of narrative, $75. Set in LISI.
Order from Seton Hall Museum; see Museums section.
_____. 30 poster illustrations (8.5"x11"), $15. (Available from Seton Hall
Museum.)
Shared Ground, 1990. Excellent 18 min. videotape focusing on the
recent oyster project on the Shinnecock Reservation in
Southampton with historical background; includes early 20th
century footage of a Southampton historic celebration. Mudfog
Films, P.O. Box 699, East Moriches, NY 11940; 878-4154. Copy in
LISI.
Suffolk County Archaeological Association (SCAA), *"Study Pictures:
Coastal Native Americans." 8.5"x11" drawings, $6. SCAA or SCHS.
_____. *"Native Technology," 26"x39" poster on material culture, $13.
SCAA or SCHS.
_____. *"Native Long Island Map," 23"x37"; Indian place names, sites
of forts, planting fields, archaeological findings, brief text. $10.
SCAA or SCHS.

Museums, Organizations, and Sources

The American Museum of Natural History in Manhattan and
the Brooklyn Museum have exhibits on Native Americans,
though they do not focus on Long Island Indians. The
Smithsonian's new National Museum of the American Indian has
exhibits in the Custom House in lower Manhattan (1 Bowling
Green; 212-668-6624).

The Friends for Long Island's Heritage, reprinted Bailey's
pamphlet; they operate museum shops at OBVR (572-8415),
Garvies Point Museum (571–8010), and St. James General Store
(862-8333). Offices are in Nassau Hall, 1864 Muttontown Road,
Syosset 11791; 571-7600.

Garvies Point Museum (Barry Road, Glen Cove) has exhibits
on Indian archaeology and regional geology; programs and
films; the museum shop has books on Indians. Call to confirm
days and hours; in 1994 open, Wed-Sat., 10-4, Sun. 1-4 (school
groups, Tues-Fri. by appointment); admission $1; 571-8010.

Long Island Studies Institute (LISI) has audiotapes of
presentations on Long Island Native Americans at its symposia
by Herbert Kraft, Gaynell Stone, Daniel Kaplan, Marguerite
Smith, James Truex, and John Strong. The Institute collections are

on the second floor of Hofstra's Library Services Center, 619 Fulton Avenue (Hempstead Turnpike/Route 24, one-half mile west of the main campus). Open to the public, Monday-Friday, 9-5 (Fridays to 4 p.m. in the summer); 463-6409/6411.

Nassau County Museum has an Anthropology Library at Sands Point Preserve in Port Washington which is open to serious students and scholars by appointment (883-1610). See also Garvies Point Museum.

Periodicals: *Long Island Forum*, 1938-date and *Long Island Historical Journal*, 1988-date.

Seton Hall University Museum, South Orange, NJ 07079; 201-761-9543 for Herbert Kraft's publications which have good illustrations and useful information adaptable for teaching about Long Island Indians.

Shinnecock Nation Museum and Cultural Center Complex, Shinnecock Reservation, PO Box 59, Southampton, NY 11969; 287-4923/4688. Plans include an exhibit hall, art gallery, and reconstruction of Shinnecock heritage village. Membership and contributions welcomed.

Southold Indian Museum. Bayview Road, Southold, 11971. Exhibits, extensive collection of artifacts, and teaching guides (see Barcel in bibliography of Teaching Materials). Open Sundays, 1:30-4:30 p.m.; 765-5500; 765-5577.

Suffolk County Archaeological Association (SCAA) has monthly meetings in Commack; publishes newsletter, posters and booklets for students (grades 4 and above), and scholarly series; conducts Long Island History Lab, summer Archaeological Field School, museum and educational programs at Hoyt Farm Park, Commack and in schools. Address: PO Drawer 1542, Stony Brook. NY 11790; 929-8725. SCAA publications are available from SCAA or at museum shops at OBVR and SCHS.

Suffolk County Historical Society, 300 W. Main Street, Riverhead: exhibit "The Indians of Eastern Long Island" and very good selection of materials in print on Long Island Indians in Weathervane Shop. For mail order sales and book list, contact the Society. Open Tuesday-Saturday, 12:30-4:30; (516) 727-2881.

Selected Bibliography of
African Americans on Long Island*

Lynda R. Day

Austin, Jere. "From the Diary of Joshua Hempstead: Slaves, Servants, and Community Service." *Long Island Forum* 22, no. 3 (March 1969): 50-51.

Boyd, Melody. "Black Population of North Hempstead: 1830-1880." Ph.D. dissertation, SUNY at Stony Brook, 1981. LISI: F129.N8B68, 1981a.

Cash, Floris Barnett. "African American Whalers: Images and Reality." *Long Island Historical Journal* 2, no. 1 (Fall 1989): 41-52.

Day, Lynda R. "Samuel Ballton." In *Between Ocean and Empire: An Illustrated History of Long Island*, ed. Robert B. MacKay et al, 94-95. Northridge, CA: Windsor Publications, 1985.

_____. *African Americans on Long Island*. Forthcoming LISI publication.

Dickerson, Glenda. "Eel Catching in Setauket: A Living Library—The African American, Christian Avenue Community." *Journal of the Three Village Historical Society*, May 1988. LISI-VF.

Eichholz, Alice and James M. Rose, *Free Black Heads of Households in the New York State Federal Census, 1790-1830*. Detroit: Gale Research, 1981. LISI.

Ernst, Robert. "A Long Island Black Tory." *Long Island Forum* 41 (January 1978): 18-19.

Goodfriend, Joyce. "Burghers and Blacks: The Evolution of a Slave Society at New Amsterdam." *New York History* 59 (April 1978): 125-44. See also her *Before the Melting Pot*, 1992.

Harris, Bradley. *Black Roots in Smithtown: A Short History of the Black Community*. Town of Smithtown: Office of the Town Historian, 1986. LISI.

James, Marquita L. "The Blacks of Roosevelt." In *Ethnicity in Suburbia: The Long Island Experience*, ed. Salvatore LaGumina, 91-94. Garden City: Nassau Community College, 1980. LISI: F127.L8E8 1980.

Kobrin, David. *The Black Minority in Early New York*. Albany: The University of the State of New York, 1971. F128.9 N3K6

Levy, Lawrence. "A Halfway House on the Way to Freedom." *Newsday*, December 10, 1980. LISI-VF.

Mabee, Carleton. *Black Education in New York State: From Colonial to Modern Times*. Syracuse: Syracuse University Press, 1979. LC2802.N7.

McKee, Samuel Jr. "Slave Labor." In *Labor in Colonial New York, 1664-1776*. New York: Columbia University Press, 1935. HD8083.

*Updated from *Exploring African-American History*, ed. Natalie A. Naylor (1991), 57-9. Call numbers are for Hofstra's Library; LISI refers to the Institute, NCM to the Nassau County Museum collection at LISI, and VF to Vertical File material.

N7M3; reprinted 1965.

McManus, Edgar J. *A History of Negro Slavery in New York.* Syracuse: Syracuse University Press, 1966. E445.N56M3.

MacMaster, Richard K. "Wilson Rantus, Negro Leader." *Long Island Forum* 25, no. 7 (July 1962): 143-44.

Marcus, Grania Bolton. *A Forgotten People: Discovering the Black Experience in Suffolk County.* Setauket: Society for the Preservation of Long Island Antiquities, 1988. LISI: E445.N56M37 1988.

_____. "A Forgotten People: Discovering the Black Experience in Suffolk County." *The Long Island Historical Journal* 1 (Fall 1988): 17-34.

Maynard, Joan and Gwen Cottman. *Weeksville, Then and Now.* Brooklyn: Society for the Preservation of Weeksville and Bedford-Stuyvesant History, 1983, 1985.

Moss, Richard Shannon. "Slavery on Long Island: Its Rise and Decline During the Seventeenth Through Nineteenth Centuries." Ph.D. dissertation, St. John's University, 1985. LISI/NCM 326.0974721. Revised and published by Garland, 1993 under the title *Slavery on Long Island: A Study in Local Institutional and Early Communal Life, 1609-1827.*

Naylor, Natalie A. ed. *Exploring African-American History.* Hempstead: Long Island Studies Institute, Hofstra University, 1991.

Olson, Edwin. "Social Aspects of Slave Life in New York." *Journal of Negro History* 26 (March 1941): 66-77.

Ransom, Stanley Austin Jr., ed. *America's First Negro Poet: The Complete Works of Jupiter Hammon.* Port Washington: Kennikat Press, 1970.

Rose, James. *A Study in Triumph: African-Americans in Queens County, New York 1683-1983.* [New York: Queens College, 1987].

Ross, Peter. "Slavery on Long Island." In *A History of Long Island From its Settlement to the Present Time,* 1: 119-33. New York: Lewis Publishing Co., 1902. Useful for lists of names reprinted from older sources.

Shodell, Elly. *It Looks Like Yesterday to Me: Port Washington's Afro-American Heritage.* Port Washington, NY: Port Washington Library, 1984. LB158.2.

Smith, Venture. *A Narrative of the Life and Adventures of Venture Smith,* [c. 1729-1805], *A Native of Africa: But Resident About Sixty Years in the United States,* 1798. Available at the Schomburg Library, New York City. Reprinted in *Five Black Lives: Autobiographies,* introduction by Arna Bontemps (Middletown, CT: Wesleyan University Press, 1970), 1-34. Excerpts in Marion Wilson Starling, *The Slave Narrative: Its Place in American History,* 2nd ed. (Washington, DC: Howard University Press, 1988), 77-84. E444.F49 and E444.S8.1988.

Swan, Robert J. "The Black Presence in Seventeenth-Century Brooklyn." *de Halve Maen,* 63 (December 1990): 1-6.

Watkins, Ralph. "A Survey of the African American Presence in the History of the Downstate New York Area." In *The African American Presence in New York State History,* ed. Monroe Fordham. (Albany: SUNY, 1989), 3-49 and 112ff (selected list of sites).

Weidman, Bette S. and Linda B. Martin. "Spinney Hill: The Hidden Community." *Long Island Forum* 43, no. 3 (March 1980): 48-55.
Wortis, Helen. "Blacks on Long Island." *Journal of Long Island History* 9 (Autumn 1974): 35-46.
____. "Black Inhabitants of Shelter Island" and "A Woman Named Matilda." In *A Woman Named Matilda And Other True Accounts of Old Shelter Island*, 19-34, 48-58. Shelter Island: The Shelter Island Historical Society, 1978. LISI: F129.S65W67.
Wood, Clarence A. "Lymas Reeve, Southold Slave." *Long Island Forum* 14, no. 8 (August 1951): 149-53; reprinted in *Long Island Forum* 51 (Spring 1988): 27-8.

Primary Sources

"Cemeteries of Wantagh" Notebook. Data on the Black Community of Smithville. Wantagh Public Library.
Florence Bates Tolliver Collection. Jericho Reference Room. Jericho Public Library.
Long Island African American Oral History Project. Port Washington Library.
"Marriage Book of 'Colored People' of Hempstead" (1874-1899). Records Room. Hempstead Town Hall.
"Negroes" vertical file. Manuscript Collection. Bryant Library, Roslyn.
Record of Children Born of Slaves. Smithtown Historical Society.
Record of Manumissions. Smithtown Historical Society.
Record of Manumissions. Town of Huntington. (Published by Town Historian.)
"Record of the Discharges of the Negroes set at liberty by Friends of Westbury Monthly Meeting" (1776-1790). Original at Haviland Records Room, New York Yearly Meeting, Society of Friends, New York City. Microfilm copy at NCM, LISI.
Salem African Church (Roslyn), Papers relative to. MacKay Collection. NCM, LISI: L62.26.3
Samuel Ballton, Papers and materials relative to. Greenlawn-Centerport Historical Society (located at the Greenlawn Public Library).
Slave bills of sale and Manumission Papers. NCM, LISI.
Youngs Family Collection. NCM, LISI: L55.29.11.

Editor's Note

The African American Museum, 110 N. Franklin St., Hempstead 11550 (572-0730) has changing exhibits and a forthcoming permanent exhibit on African Americans on Long Island.

Grania Marcus's *A Forgotten People: Discovering the Black Experience in Suffolk County* (1988), reprints documents and has questions designed for secondary students. See also *Exploring African-American History*, ed. Natalie A. Naylor (1991) which includes Dr. Marcus's essay, "Discovering the African-American Experience on Long Island" (1–20), Floris Barnett Cash's "Long Island's African-American Women" (25–30), shorter essays on Weeksville and Lewis Latimer, and materials for researchers and teachers including "Manuscripts, Census Data, and Articles on African-American History: Samples and Suggestions for Using in the Classroom" (31–48), by Natalie A. Naylor and Dorothy B. Ruettgers, "Incorporating African-American History into the Elementary Curriculum" (49–55) by Jeanne Murray, and bibliographies (57–63).

In the Joseph Lloyd Manor House in Lloyd Harbor, SPLIA interprets the experiences of Jupiter Hammon, the first African-American poet (call 941-9444 for hours). See Wendy Abel-weiss. "Slavery in Our House," *History News* 41 (February 1985): 20-21 (copy in LISI-VF).

SPLIA's pre-visit videotapes, *Joseph Lloyd Manor House*, (11 mins., 1986) and *Long Island Slavery: Six Portraits*, (12 mins. 1991) can be viewed at the Long Island Studies Institute. See also "Uncovering a Forgotten People: Slaves of Lloyd Manor and 18th century Suffolk County," a pre-visit booklet of curriculum materials (in the Curriculum Materials Center in Hostra's Axinn Library and in LISI). SPLIA's poster, "The Black Experience on Long Island," has a map and time line illustrating where important events took place and where African Americans lived.

On black cemeteries in Wantagh, Copiague, and Matinecock, see: Karl F. Pfeiffer, *Old Burying Ground* (Wantagh American Revolution Bicentennial Committee, 1975); "Historic Black Cemetery to Be Restored," *Newsday*, October 24, 1979; and "A Graveyard Restored," *Locust Valley Leader*, November 29, 1990. (Old African-American cemeteries are often near black churches.)

Some of the issues of *The Journal of Historical Inquiry* have articles on African Americans in Amityville by Amityville High School students; copies are in the Long Island Studies Institute. (See essay by Charles Howlett, supra.) The *Journal of Negro History* and *Afro-Americans in New York Life and History* are periodicals which may be useful resources. Linda Grant DePauw's pamphlet, *Four Traditions: Women of New York During the American Revolution* (1974), discusses Iroquois, Dutch, African, and English women in the colony of New York.

Long Island Women: Bibliography

"Alicia [Patterson] in Wonderland," *Time,* September 13, 1954. See also Robert F. Keeler, *Newsday: A Candid History of the Respectable Tabloid,* 1990.

Bailey, Paul. "Famous L.I. Women." *Long Island Press,* July 29 and August 3, 1961.

Baxandall, Rosalyn and Elizabeth Ewen. "Picture Windows: The Changing Role of Women in the Suburbs, 1945-2000." *Long Island Historical Journal* 3 (Fall 1990): 89-108.

Biemer, Linda. "Lady Deborah Moody and the Founding of Gravesend." *The Journal of Long Island History* 17 (1981): 24-42.

Black Women of Brooklyn. Brooklyn Historical Society, 1985. Exhibit catalog.

Bland, Sidney R. "'Never Quite So Committed as We'd Like': The Suffrage Militancy of Lucy Burns." *The Journal of Long Island History* 17 (1981): 4-23.

Capozzoli, Mary Jane. *Three Generations of Italian American Women in Nassau County, New York, 1925-1981.* New York: Garland, 1990.

Cash, Floris Barnett. "Long Island's African-American Women," in *Exploring African-American History,* ed. Natalie A. Naylor (Hempstead: LISI, 1991), 53-7.

Custead, Alma. "Elizabeth Oakes-Smith, Period Piece." *Long Island Forum,* 4 (February 1941): 27-8.

Dyson, Verne. *The Human Story of Long Island,* 1969. Includes Lady Deborah Moody, Anna Harrison, Julia Gardiner Tyler, Jacqueline Kennedy, and Margaret Fuller.

Flick, Alexander. "Lady Deborah Moody: Grand Dame of Gravesend." *Long Island Historical Society Quarterly* 1 (July 1929): 69-75.

Floyd, Candace. "Legend vs. History: Raynham Hall Redirects Interpretation [of Sally Townsend] from Romance to Documentary." *History News* 36 (September 1981): 14-15.

Hicks, Rachel. *Memoir of Rachel Hicks,* 1880. Quaker minister (1789-1878).

Horne, Field, ed. *The Diary of Mary Cooper: Life on a Long Island Farm, 1768-1773,* 1983. Excerpts in June Sprigg, ed. *Domestic Beings,* 1984.

Keller, Evelyn Fox. *A Feeling for the Organism: The Life and Work of Barbara McClintock,* 1983. Nobel laureate scientist who worked at Cold Spring Harbor Laboratory for a half century

Koppelman, Lucille L. "Lady Deborah Moody and Gravesend 1643-1659." *de Halve Maen* 67 (Summer 1992):38-43.

Lee, Josette. "Our Founding Mothers . . . an Exercise in Domestic Feminism," *The Quarterly of the Huntington Historical Society* 16 (Fall/Winter 1986): 7-28.

Leoniak, Mallory and Jane S. Gombieski. *To Get the Votes: Woman Suffrage Leaders in Suffolk County.* Town of Brookhaven, 1992.

Lockwood, Estelle D. "The Lady Known as '355.'" *Long Island Forum* 55 (Winter 1993): 10-15. New evidence challenges the legend of the Revolutionary war spy.

Lynn [Gerber], Joanne. "'Women's Cradle of Aviation': Curtiss Field, Valley Stream," in *Evoking a Sense of Place*, ed. Joann P. Krieg (Interlaken, Heart of the Lakes: 1988), 85-95.

Mathews, Jane. "'General' Rosalie Jones, Long Island Suffragist," *Nassau County Historical Society Journal* 47 (1992): 23-34.

_____. "The Woman Suffrage Movement in Suffolk County, New York, 1911-1917: A Case Study of the Tactical Differences Between Two Prominent Long Island Suffragists: Mrs. Ida Bunce Sammis and Miss Rosalie Jones." M.A. thesis, Adelphi University, 1986. (Copy in LISI.) Audiotape of Mathews' March 1987 talk on Long Island suffrage is in LISI.

MacKay, Ann, ed. *She Went A-Whaling: The Journal of Martha Smith Brewer Brown, 1847–1849*. Orient, NY: Oysterponds Historical Society, 1993.

McGee, Dorothy Horton. *Sally Townsend, Patriot,* 1952.

Metz, Clinton. "Sarah Ann Baldwin Barnum." *Long Island Forum* 57 (1984): 167-73.

Morris, Sylvia. *Edith Kermit Roosevelt: Portrait of a First Lady,* 1980.

Naylor, Natalie A. "Long Island's Mrs. Tippecanoe and Mrs. Tyler Two." *Long Island Historical Journal* 6 (Fall 1993): 2-16.

_____. "Long Island's Notable Women," *Long Island Forum* 47 (June and July, 1984): 104-9, 135-9.

_____. "Mary Steichen Calderone." In *Women Educators in the United States, 1820-1993,* ed. Maxine Schwartz Seller (Westport: Greenwood, 1994): 86-94.

Quinn, Sr. Margaret. "Sylvia, Adele, and Rosine Parmentier: Nineteenth Century Women of Brooklyn." *U.S. Catholic Historian* 4 (1986): 345-4. The Parmentier papers are in the Archives, St. Joseph Convent, Brentwood, NY.

Smith, Elinor. *Aviatrix,* 1981. Autobiography of a pioneer Long Island aviator.

Smith, Mildred H. "The Remarkable Mrs. Stewart." *Garden City News,* April 19, 1985.

Spinzia, Raymond E. "In Her Wake: The Story of Alva Smith Vanderbilt Belmont." *The Long Island Historical Journal* 6 (Fall 1993): 96-105.

Stone, Gaynell. "Women's Work: Native and African Americans of Long Island." Exhibit leaflet [1993].

Strong, Lara M. and Selcuk Karabag. "Quashawam: Sunksquaw of the Montauk." *Long Island Historical Journal* 3 (Spring 1991): 189-204.

Strasser, Susan. *Never Done: History of American Housework,* 1982. Re Christine Frederick, 214-9, 246-50.

Thwaite, Ann. *Waiting for the Party: The Life of Frances Hodgson Burnett, 1849-1924,* 1974. Phyllis Bixler and Vivian Burnett have also written biographies; see also Burnett's autobiography and children's biographies by Constance Burnett (1965) and Angelica Carpenter and Jean Shirley, *Beyond the Secret Garden,* 1990.

Valentine, Harriet G. *The Window to the Street: A Mid-Ninteenth-Century View of Cold Spring Harbor, New York, Based on the Diary of Helen Rogers*, 1981. Reprint; Cold Spring Harbor: Whaling Museum, 1991.

Weigold, Marilyn. *Silent Builder: Emily Warren Roebling and the Brooklyn Bridge*, 1984.

_____. "Montauk's Angels: The Women's War Relief Association at Camp Wikoff (1898)," *Long Island Forum* 48 (Oct. 1985): 191-5; and "1911 Crop of Female Farmers," *Long Island Forum* 43 (June 1980): 116-24.

Wilhelm, Arlene. "Quaker Women of Westbury and Jericho," 1981. Senior project, SUNY College at Old Westbury. Copy at Historical Society of the Westburys, Long Island History Collection, Cottage, Westbury Library.

Wittenburg, Joy. "Excerpts from the Diary of Elizabeth Oakes Smith," *Signs* 9 (Spring 1984): 534-48.

Wortis, Helen Zunser. *A Woman Named Matilda and Other True Accounts of Old Shelter Island*, 1978. Matilda was a slave manumitted in 1795.

Yeager, Edna H. "Long Island's Unsung." *Daughters of the American Revolution Magazine* 109 (October 1975): 908-14. Also "Long Island Women in the Revolution," *Long Island Forum* 40 (Jan. 1977): 10-11.

See also sources cited in *Notable American Women* for women listed in "Nationally Notable Long Island Women" which follows the section on "Important Long Islanders."

Important Long Islanders*

Abraham, Abraham (1843-1911), Brooklyn. Founder of Abraham and Straus, philanthropist.

Adams, James Truslow (1878-1949), Bridgehampton. Historian.

Armstrong, Louis (1901-1971), Corona. Jazz musician.

Bailey, Paul (died 1962), Amityville. Historian and founding editor *Long Island Forum*.

Ballton, Samuel (1838-1917), Greenlawn. Black entrepreneur, "Pickle King."

Barnum, Sarah Baldwin (Mrs. Peter C., 1814-1893), East Meadow. Civic leader.

Bassett, Preston R. (1892-1992), Rockville Centre. Engineer (1914-) and president (1945-1956) Sperry Gyroscope Company.

Beecher, Henry Ward (1813-1887), Brooklyn. Minister.

Beecher, Lyman (1775-1863), East Hampton. Minister.

Belmont, August Sr. (1816-1890), Babylon. Banker, sportsman.

Belmont, Jr., August (1853-1924), Hempstead and Babylon. Investment banker and horsebreeder.

Benson, Egbert, (1746-1833), Jamaica. Judge.

Birdsall, Col. Benjamin (1736-1798), Hempstead. Fought in Revolutionary War, Assemblyman.

Blakelock, Ralph (1847-1919), Blue Point. General in Salvation Army.

Booth, Ballington (1857-1920), Blue Point. Founder and Commander, Volunteers of America.

Bowne, John (c. 1628-1695), Flushing. Quaker persecuted in 1662.

Brewster, Caleb (1747-1827), Setauket. Member of spy ring.

Bryant, William Cullen (1794-1878), Roslyn. Poet and editor, *New York Evening Post* (1829-1878).

Buell, Rev. Samuel (1716-1798), East Hampton. Minister and founder Clinton Academy, 1784.

Calderone, Mary (1904-), Great Neck and Glen Head. Sex educator.

Carpenter, Joseph (c. 1635-1683), and family, Glen Cove. Chief proprietor.

Chase, William Merritt (1849-1916), Southampton. Artist and art teacher.

---

*See also list of "Nationally Notable Long Island Women" (NNLIW) below whose names are not repeated here. These lists are not exhaustive and are more limited on persons still active in their careers. The designation "Long Islander" includes some who were summer residents or had relatively brief sojourns (e.g. F. Scott Fitzgerald and Charles Lindbergh), but all lived or worked on the Island during their years of accomplishment. Long Island is defined geographically, including Queens and Brooklyn as well as Nassau and Suffolk. There are many books on the most famous Long Islanders (Theodore Roosevelt and Walt Whitman), but information on less well-known individuals may be difficult to find. Dan Rattiner, *Who's Here: The Heart of the Hamptons* (Wainscott: Pushcart Press, 1994), includes many contemporary celebrities who reside in the Hamptons.

Childs, John Lewis (1856-1921), Floral Park (founder). Seed business.
Coles, Robert (197-1985), Glen Cove. Naturalist, astronomer, and Long Island historian.
Cooper, James Fenimore (1789-1854), Sag Harbor (1819-23). Novelist.
Cooper, Mary [Molly] (1714-1778), Oyster Bay. Farmwife, diarist (1768-1773).
Cooper, Peter (1792-1883), Hempstead (1812-1818). Inventor and philanthropist.
Corbin, Austin (1827-1896), Deer Park. Deveoped Manhattan Beach (Coney Island) and president of Long Island Railroad, 1880-1896.
Cuffee, Paul (1757-1812), Canoe Place and Montauk. Indian minister.
Curtiss, Glenn (1878-1930). Pioneer aviator (Hempstead Plains) and plane manufacturer, factory in Garden City (1918-1931).
Cutter, Bloodgood (1817-1906), Great Neck. Mill owner, Mark Twain immortalized as "Poet Lariat."
D'Amato, Alfonse (1937-), Island Park. U.S. Senator.
Dana, Charles A. (1819-1897), Glen Cove. Newspaper editor, summer resident.
Davis, John W. (1873-1955), Locust Valley (country home). Lawyer, diplomat, Democratic candidate for President, 1924.
Davis, William M. (1829-1920), Port Jefferson. Artist.
Davis, William Steeple (1884-1916), Orient Point. Painter.
Davison, Trubee (1896-1974), Locust Valley. Organized Yale unit of naval aviators in World War I, governmental official.
de Kooning, Elaine (1920-1989), East Hampton. Painter.
de Kooning, Willem (1904-), Springs and East Hampton. Abstract expressionist painter.
Dering, Henry Packer (1763-1822), Sag Harbor. Customs agent 1790-1822.
Dominy, Nathaniel (1737-1812) and family (active 1714-1868), East Hampton. Cabinet makers.
Doubleday, Frank Nelson (1862-1934), Nelson Doubleday, Sr. (1889-1949), and Nelson Doubleday, Jr. (1933-), Mill Neck and Locust Valley, business in Garden City. Book publishers. Nelson Doubleday, Jr., owner, New York Mets baseball team.
Doughty, G. Wilbur (died 1930), Inwood. Republican legislator, party leader.
Drew, John (1853-1927), East Hampton. Actor.
Embury, Aymar, II (1880-1966), East Hampton. Architect.
Erving, Julius ("Dr. J.," 1950-), Roosevelt. Basketball player with New York Nets.
Feke, Robert (1705-1750), Oyster Bay. Portrait painter.
Ferraro, Geraldine (1935-), Forest Hills. Member of Congress, first woman nominated for vice president of U.S. (1984) on major party ticket.
Field, Marshall, III (1893-1956), "Caumsett," Lloyd Neck. Publisher and corporate director.
Fitzgerald, F. Scott (1896-1940), Great Neck in 1923-1924. Author *Great Gatsby* describing Gold Coast.

Floyd, William (1734-1821), Mastic. Signer of the Declaration of Independence.
Folger, Henry (1857-1930), Brooklyn and Glen Cove. Collector of Shakespeariana. (See also Emily Folger in NNLIW.)
Friedan, Betty (1921-), Great Neck, Sag Harbor. Feminist author.
Frothingham, David, Sag Harbor. Editor, published first Long Island newspaper, 1791-1798.
Fullerton, Edith (Mrs. Hal B., 1876-1931), Huntington, Wading River, Medford. Writer on horticulture and agriculture.
Fullerton, Hal B. (1857-1935), Huntington, Wading River, Medford. Special agent and photographer for Long Island Railroad, 1897-1927.
Furman, Gabriel (1800-1854), Brooklyn. Public official and historian.
Gardiner family; Lion Gardiner (1599-1663), Gardiners Island, East Hampton. Early settlers; island has remained in family to present.
Green, Isaac Henry (1858-1937), Sayville. Architect.
Grumman, Leroy (1895-1982), Plandome. Founder of Grumman Aircraft Corporation.
Guggenheim, Harry (1890-1971), Sands Point (Falaise). Financed aviation research and publisher *Newsday.*
Guy, Francis (1760-1820), Brooklyn. Painter.
Hall, Leonard W. (1900-1979), Oyster Bay and Locust Valley. Congressman (1939-1953) and Republican National Chairman (1953-1957).
Hammon, Jupiter (1711-c. 1800), Lloyd Neck. African-American poet.
Hassam, Childe (1859-1935), East Hampton (1877-1900). Artist.
Heckscher, August (1848-1941), Huntington. Business executive and philanthropist (Heckscher Park and Museum in Huntington and Heckscher State Park).
Hewitt, Mattie Edwards (died 1956). Photographed Long Island estates (1909-1930s).
Hicks, Elias (1748-1830), Jericho. Quaker preacher.
Hicks, Isaac (1767-1820), Westbury. New York City merchant.
Hicks, Rachel (1789-1878), Westbury. Quaker preacher.
Hicks, Rachel (1857-1941), Roslyn. Photographer.
Hobart, John Sloss (1738-1805), Eaton's Neck. Patriot, judge, senator.
Homer, Winslow (1836-1910), East Hampton. Painter.
Jones, John H. (1785-1859), Cold Spring Harbor. Founded whaling company 1837.
Jones, Rosalie Gardner (1883-1978), Cold Spring Harbor. Suffragist.
Jones, Samuel (1734-1819), West Neck, Oyster Bay. Public official, delegate to New York State's ratifying Convention for U.S. Constitution.
Jones, Walter Restored (1793-1855), Cold Spring Harbor. Marine insurance executive, financed whaling fleet.
Kahn, Otto (1867-1934), "Oheka" Cold Spring Harbor. Banker, art patron.
King, Rufus (1755-1827), Jamaica (King Manor, 1803-1827). Public official.
Krasner, Lee (1908-1984), East Hampton. Painter.

Lange, Edward (1846-1912), Greenlawn. Artist.
Latimer, Lewis (1848-1928), Flushing. Inventor worked with Thomas Edison.
Levitt, William J. (1907-1994). Builder and developer of Levittown (1947-1951); Levitt firm had built houses in Rockville Centre and the Strathmore developments in Roslyn and Manhasset in the 1930s.
Lewis, Francis (1713-1803), Whitestone. Signer of Declaration of Independence.
L'Hommedieu, Ezra (1734-1811), Southold. Public official and Regent.
Lindbergh, Charles A. (1902-1974). Aviator, first to fly solo non-stop across Atlantic (from Roosevelt Field), 1927.
Lloyd family, Lloyd Neck. Henry Lloyd I (1685-1763) and Joseph Lloyd (1716-1680) were early settlers on the "Manor of Queens Village"; homes are preserved.
Lombardo, Guy (1902-1977), Freeport. Orchestra leader, produced shows at Jones Beach Theatre.
Loughlin, John (1817-1891), Brooklyn. Catholic bishop.
Low, Abiel Abbot (1811-1893), Brooklyn. Merchant and civic leader.
Low, Seth (1850-1916), Brooklyn. Mayor Brooklyn and New York City.
Luke, Myron G. (1905-), West Hempstead. Long Island historian and Editor, *The Nassau County Historical Society Journal* (1950-).
Mackay, Clarence H. (1874-1938), Roslyn. Industrialist and philanthropist.
Mackay, Katherine Duer (Mrs. Clarence, 1879-1930), Roslyn. Suffragist.
McClintock, Barbara (1902-1992), Cold Spring Harbor. Geneticist, Nobel Prize winner.
McKinney-Steward, Dr. Susan Smith (1847-1918), Brooklyn. First black woman physician in New York.
McLaughlin, Hugh (1826-1904), Brooklyn. Democratic political boss.
Macy, W. Kingsland (1891-1961), Islip. Suffolk Republican leader (1926-1951).
Merritt, Jesse (1889-1957), Farmingdale. Long Island historian.
Miller, Charles Henry (1842-1922), Queens. Painter.
Mitchell, Samuel Latham (1764-1831), Plandome. Scientist, public official.
Moody, Lady Deborah (c. 1583-1659?), Gravesend. Founder and chief patentee.
Moran, Thomas (1837-1926), East Hampton. Artist. (Wife, Mary Moran, is in NNLIW.)
Morgan, J. P., Jr. (John Pierpont, 1867-1943), Centre Island. Investment banker and philanthropist.
Morley, Christopher (1890-1957), Roslyn. Author, critic.
Moses, Robert (1888-1981), Babylon. State park commissioner; built bridges, parks, and parkways.
Motherwell, Robert (1915-1951), East Hampton. Abstract expressionist artist.
Mount, Shepherd Alonzo (1804-1868), Stony Brook. Artist.

Mount, William Sidney (1807-1868), Stony Brook. Artist.
Mulford, Samuel (1644-1725), East Hampton. Merchant.
Murphy, Robert Cushman (1887-1973), Setauket. Naturalist, author.
Occom, Samson (1723-1792), Montauk. Missionary, school for Indians.
Paulding, Admiral Hiram (1797-1878), Huntington. Naval officer and
    head of Brooklyn Navy Yard.
Payne, John Howard (1792-1852), East Hampton. Wrote "Home Sweet
    Home."
Pelletreau, Elias (1726-1810) and family, Southampton. Silversmiths.
Pennypacker, Morton (1872-1956), East Hampton. Historian and book
    collector.
Pharoah, Stephen, a.k.a. Stephen Talkhouse (1819-1879), East
    Hampton and Montauk. Montauk whaler, hunter, and walker.
Pierrepont, Hezekiah B. (1768-1838), Brooklyn. Developer of Brooklyn
    Heights.
Pollock, Jackson (1912-1956), Springs/East Hampton. Abstract
    expressionist artist.
Porter, Fairfield (1907-1975), Southampton. Painter.
Pratt, Charles (1830-1891), Brooklyn and Glen Cove. Standard Oil
    Company executive and philanthropist (Pratt Institute).
Prince family, William (c. 1725-1802) William (1766-1842) and William
    Robert (1795-1869), Flushing. Nurserymen and authors, founded
    Linnaean Botanic Gardens.
Quimby, Harriet (1884-1912). First licensed woman pilot, learned to
    fly on Hempstead Plains.
Raiche, Bessica (active 1910s), Mineola. First American woman to pilot
    an airplane.
Roebling, John (1806-1869), Washington (1837-1926), and Emily
    (1843-1903), Brooklyn. Brooklyn Bridge engineers.
Rogers, Nathaniel (1787-1844), Bridgehampton. Artist (miniaturist).
Roosevelt, Theodore (1858-1919), Oyster Bay. President of the United
    States. See NNLIW for wife, Edith Roosevelt.
Samis, Ida Bunce (1868-1913), Huntington. Suffragist, one of the first
    women elected to the New York Assembly.
Schiff, Dorothy (1903-1989), East Norwich. Publisher, *New York Post.*
Scott, John (1634?-1696), Setauket and Southampton. Self-proclaimed
    "President" of Long Island, 1663.
Selijns, Henricus (1636-1701), Brooklyn. Dutch Reformed clergyman.
Smith, Elinor (Sullivan, 1911-), Freeport. Pioneer aviator.
Smythe, Richard (died 1692), and Smith family, Smithtown. Founder
    and patentee.
Sousa, John Phillip (1854-1932), Sands Point. Composer and band
    leader.
Sperry, Elmer (1860-1930), Bellport. Inventor and engineer.
Sperry, Laurence (1892-1923), Brooklyn and Farmingdale. Inventor
    and engineer.
Sprague, J. Russell (1886-1969). Nassau County Republican leader.
Stafford, Jean (Liebling, 1915-1979), East Hampton. Author.
Stewart, Alexander T. (1803-1876), Garden City. Founder of Garden
    City.

Stewart, Cornelia Clinch (Mrs. Alexander T. , 1805?-1886), Garden City. Philanthropist.

Stewart, T. McCants, (1854-1923), Brooklyn. Black lawyer.

Stiles, Henry R. (1832-1909), Brooklyn. Doctor and historian.

Stimson, Henry L. (1867-1950), Huntington. U.S. Secretary of State.

Stranahan, James (1808-1898), Brooklyn. Civic leader, founder of Prospect Park.

Strong, Anna or Nancy (1740-1812), Setauket. Aided spy ring in Revolutionary War.

Strong, Kate (1879-1977), Setauket. Historian.

Tackapousha (17th century). Indian sachem.

Tallmadge, Col. Benjamin (1754-1835), Brookhaven. Revolutionary war hero.

Thompson, Benjamin (1784-1849), Hempstead. Historian.

Thompson, John T. (1860-1940) , Great Neck. Engineer, invented Thompson submachine gun ("Tommy gun").

Tiffany, Louis Comfort (1848-1933), Cold Spring Harbor. Designed and produced stained glass; factory in Corona.

Townsend, Samuel (1717-1790) and family, Oyster Bay. Merchants, spy ring.

Underhill, Capt. John (1597-1672), Flushing and Oyster Bay. Colonial official and Indian fighter.

Vanderbilt, William K. (Sr., 1849-1920), Oakdale ("Idle Hour"). Capitalist, railroad magnet.

Vanderbilt, William K. (Jr., 1878-1944), Lake Success and Centerport ("Eagles Nest"). Railroad magnet; built Long Island Motor Parkway.

Viscardi, Henry, Jr. (1912-), Kings Point. Founder Abilities.

Warhol, Andy (1930-1987), Montauk. Artist.

Watson, James (1928-), Cold Spring Harbor. Biologist, Nobel Prize winner, Director of Cold Spring Harbor Laboratory (1968-1993), President (1993-).

White, Stanford (1853-1906), Smithtown. Architect (McKim, Mead and White).

Whitman, Walt (1819-1892), West Hills (Huntington Station) and Brooklyn. Poet.

Whitney, John Hay "Jock" (1904-), Manhasset. Publisher *New York Herald Tribune*, Ambassador to England.

Willis, Benjamin, Roslyn (1840-1886). Civil War officer.

Woodhull, General Nathaniel (1722-1775), Mastic. Revolutionary War hero.

Wyandanch (died 1659). Indian sachem.

Nationally Notable Long Island Women*

Adams, Maude (1872-1953), Ronkonkoma. Actress.

Alexander, Hattie Elizabeth (1901-1968), Port Washington. Pediatrics professor and medical researcher at Columbia Presbyterian.

Ayres, Sister Anne (1816-1896), Queens and Kings Park. First woman in America to become an Episcopal sister; began religious order; worked with Dr. William Augustus Muhlenberg.

Bancroft, Jessie Hubbell (1867-1952), Brooklyn and Queens. Physical education teacher and administrator, Brooklyn and New York City school systems.

Bayer, Adèle Parmentier (1814-1892), Brooklyn. Pioneer Catholic welfare worker; known as the "Guardian Angel of the Sailors" for her work with merchant seamen.

Belmont, Alva Erskine Smith Vanderbilt (1853-1933), Sands Point and East Meadow. Suffragist.

Blatch, Harriot Eaton Stanton, (1856-1940), Shoreham. Suffragist.

Boole, Ella Alexander (1858-1952), Brooklyn. Temperance leader; President, Women's Christian Temperance Union, 1915-1933.

Bremer, Edith Terry (1885-1964), Port Washington. Leader in immigrant social service work; founder, International Institute movement.

Brownscombe, Jennie Augusta (1850-1936), Bayside. Painter specializing in genre and historical scenes.

Burchenal, Elizabeth (1876?-1959), Brooklyn. Folk dance educator; founder Folk Dance Society.

Burnett, Frances Hodgson (1849-1924), Plandome. Author *Secret Garden* and other popular books (including *Sara Crewe or A Little Princess* and *Little Lord Fauntleroy*).

Burns, Lucy (1879-1966), Brooklyn. Leader in militant wing of suffrage movement; worked with Alice Paul; chief organizer in Congressional Union and National Women's Party.

Campbell, Persia Crawford (1898-1974), Queens. Economics professor, Queens College, 1939-1965; consumer advocate in New York State government and United Nations; a Director of Consumers Union.

Cary, Elisabeth Luther (1867-1936), Brooklyn. First full-time art critic of the *New York Times* (1908-1936); writer on art and literature.

---

*Limited to women who lived or worked on Long Island for extended periods (including their years of achievement) who appear in the standard scholarly reference works: *Notable American Women, 1607-1950: A Biographical Dictionary*, edited by Edward T. James et al., 3 vols. (Cambridge: Harvard University Press, 1971) and Supplement, *Notable American Women The Modern Period*, edited by Barbara Sicherman and Carol Hurd Green (Cambridge: Harvard University Press, 1980). For inclusion, women must have died before 1976; Barbara McClintock (1902-1992) will certainly be in a future supplement. See also Natalie A. Naylor, "Long Island's Notable Women," *Long Island Forum* 47 (June and July, 1984): 104-9, 135-9. These sources include bibliographic references; see also "Long Island Women: Bibliography" above.

Castle, Irene (1893-1969), Manhasset. Fashion-setting dancer; with husband, Vincent, in 1910s popularized tango, Castle Polka, and Hesitation Walk.

Crosby, Fanny (1820-1915), Brooklyn. Author of more than five thousand hymns.

Dennett, Mary Coffin Ware (1872-1947), Astoria. Officer, suffrage associations; active advocate of birth control and sex education who challenged Comstock and other restrictive laws.

Doubleday, Neltje Blanchan De Graff (1865-1918), Locust Valley. Author of bird and garden books, under pen name, Neltje Blanchan.

Dreier, Mary Elisabeth (1875-1963), Brooklyn. Headed New York Trade Union League; active in suffrage and peace movements and in labor reform.

Earle, Alice Morse (1851-1911), Brooklyn. Author *Home Life in Colonial Days* and other books on colonial social history,

Fedde, Sister Elizabeth (1850-1921), Brooklyn. Founder Lutheran nurses training center and hospital in Brooklyn (now Lutheran Medical Center).

Folger, Emily Clara Jordan (1858-1936), Brooklyn and Glen Cove. Collaborated with husband in assembling Shakespeare collection; founders of Folger Shakespeare Library in Washington, DC.

Frederick, Christine McGaffey (1883-1970), Greenlawn. Household efficiency expert, author, and editor; operated Applecroft Home Experiment Station.

Garnet, Sarah J. Smith Thompson (1831-1911), Brooklyn (roots in Hempstead). First black principal in New York City public schools; active in suffrage organizations.

Harrison, Anna Symmes (1775-1864), grew up in Southold. Wife of William Henry Harrison and grandmother of Benjamin Harrison, United States presidents.

Havemeyer, Louise Waldron Elder (1855-1929), Bay Shore. Art collector, suffragist, and philanthropist.

Hunton, Addie D. Waites (1875-1943), Brooklyn. Black leader and Young Women's Christian Association (YWCA) official.

Keller, Helen (1880-1968), Forest Hills (1917-1939). Author; advocate, role model, and fund-raiser for handicapped (Keller was deaf, blind, and mute from 19 months of age).

Kober, Alice Elizabeth (1906-1950), Brooklyn. Classics scholar, Brooklyn College; deciphered Linear B.

Levine, Lena (1903-1965), Brooklyn. Gynecologist and psychiatrist; active in birth control movement and marriage and sex counseling.

Libbey, Laura Jean (1862-1925), Brooklyn. Author of romantic novels.

Matthews, Victoria Earle (1861-1907), Brooklyn. Founder National Association of Colored Women and the White Rose Mission which provided vocational training for young black girls.

Miller, Olive Thorne (1831-1918), Brooklyn. Author of children's stories and books on birds.

Moody, Lady Deborah (c. 1583-1659?), Gravesend. Founder of Gravesend in 1643, the first English settlement in western Long Island.

Moore, Marianne (1887-1972), Brooklyn. Poet, literary critic, editor.

Moran, Mary Nimmo (1842-1899), East Hampton. Painter and etcher.

Morgan, Helen (1900?-1941), Brooklyn. Popular singer and actress; played Julie in *Show Boat* on stage and film.

Mosher, Elizabeth Maria (1846-1928), Brooklyn. Physician; promoted health services and physical education for college women.

Ovington, Mary White (1865-1951), Brooklyn. A founder and officer, NAACP.

Palmer, Frances [Fanny] Flora Bond (1812-1876), Brooklyn. Artist and lithographer; one of the most prolific artists for Currier & Ives firm; some of her lithographs are Long Island scenes.

Patterson, Alicia (1906-1963), Sands Point. A founder (1940), co-publisher (with husband, Harry Guggenheim), and editor of *Newsday*.

Plummer, Mary Wright (1856-1916), Brooklyn. Head of Pratt Library School, 1894-1911 and New York Public Library School, 1911-1916; advocated better training for librarians.

Post, Marjorie Merriweather (1887-1973), "Hillwood," Brookville (now C. W. Post College). Businesswoman (General Foods).

Powdermaker, Hortense (1896-1970), Queens. Anthropology professor, Queens College, 1938-1968; author *Hollywood: The Dream Factory* (1950) and *Stranger and Friend: The Way of an Anthropologist* (1966).

Powell, Maude (1868-1920), Great Neck. Concert violinist.

Preston, May Wilson (1873-1949), East Hampton. Popular illustrator; member of "Ashcan School"; exhibited at 1913 Armory Show.

Rand, Marie Gertrude (1886-1970), Stony Brook. Researcher in physiological optics.

Rathbone, Josephine Adam (1864-1941), Brooklyn. Teacher Pratt Library School from 1890; Head of Pratt Library School, 1911-1938; President, American Library Association, 1931-1932.

Ray, Charlotte (1850-1911), Brooklyn and Woodside, Queens. First African-American woman lawyer; taught in Brooklyn public schools.

Roosevelt, Edith Kermit Carow (1861-1948), Oyster Bay. Theodore Roosevelt's second wife and "a most impressive" First Lady, 1901-1909.

Sabin (Davis), Pauline Morton (1887-1955), Southampton. Republican party official; active in repeal of prohibition.

Sage, Margaret Olivia Slocum (1828-1918), country homes in Lawrence and Sag Harbor. Philanthropist; many of her gifts were memorials to her husband, Russell Sage.

Sangster, Margaret Elizabeth Munson (1838-1912), Brooklyn. Magazine editor and author, *Hearth and Home* and *Harper's Bazaar* (1889-1899).

Smith, Elizabeth Oakes Prince (1806-1893), Patchogue. Author and
    reformer; poet and novelist; writer and lecturer on women's
    rights (e.g. *Women and Her Needs*).
Sullivan, Mary Josephine Quinn (1877-1939), Brooklyn and Astoria.
    Art collector and teacher; a founder of the Museum of Modern
    Art; operated art gallery.
Thursby, Emma Cecilia (1845-1931), Brooklyn. Concert singer and
    vocal teacher.
Tyler, Julia Gardiner (1820-1889), East Hampton. Second wife of U.S.
    President John Tyler and First Lady, 1844-1845.
Wheeler, Candace Thurber (1827-1923), Brooklyn and Jamaica. Textile
    designer (embroidered tapestries) and interior decorator; worked
    for Tiffany Associated Artists (1879-83); formed own Associated
    Artists, 1883-90.
Whitney, Gertrude Vanderbilt (1875-1942), Westbury. Sculptor, art
    patron, and founder of the Whitney Museum of Art.
Wolfson, Theresa (1897-1972), Brooklyn. Labor economist; professor,
    Brooklyn College, 1928-1967; specialized in labor relations; author
    Women Workers and the Trade Unions.

Long Island Historical Societies and Organizations

Most groups have regular meetings and special events; some have historical museums. Many groups rely on volunteers and telephone numbers may change; the public library may be able to provide information on the local historical society. A list of some Long Island environmental groups is appended.

Amagansett Historical Association, PO Box 7077 (Windmill Lane), Amagansett, NY 11930; 516-267-3020/267-6835.

Amityville Historical Society, PO Box 764 (Lauder Museum, 170 Broadway), Amityville, NY 11701; 516-598-1486.

Astoria (Greater), Historical Society, 35-20 Broadway, Astoria, NY 11106; 718-721-9000.

Babylon Village Historical and Preservation Society, PO Box 484 (117 Main St.), Babylon, NY 11702; 516-669-1756/669-7086/669-7766.

Baldwin Historical Society and Museum, 1980 Grand Ave., Baldwin, NY 11510; 516-223-6900.

Bayport Heritage Association, PO Box 4, Bayport, NY 11705; 516-472-9395.

Bay Shore Historical Society, 22 Maple Avenue, Bay Shore, NY 11706.

Bayside Historical Society, PO Box 133 (Fort Totten), Bayside, NY 11361; 718-224-5707.

Bayville Historical Society, 34 School St., Bayville, NY 11709; 516-628-1720.

Bellmores, Historical Society of, 32 Stratford Court, North Bellmore, NY 11710; 516-826-0333/221-4222.

Bellport-Brookhaven Historical Society, 31 Bellport Lane, Bellport, NY 11713; 516-286-0888.

Bethpage. Central Park Historical Society, PO Box 178, Bethpage, NY 11714.

Bohemia Historical Society, PO Box 67, Bohemia, NY 11716; 567-1095.

Bowne House Historical Society, 37-01 Bowne St., Flushing, NY 11354; 718-359-0528.

Bridgehampton Historical Society and Museum, PO Box 1119 (Main Street), Bridgehampton, NY 11932; 516-537-1088.

Brookhaven Town Historical Society, PO Box 613, Selden, NY 11784-0987.

Brooklyn Historical Society, 128 Pierrepont St., Brooklyn, NY 11201; 718-624-0890.

Cedar Swamp Historical Society, Cedar Swamp (Glen Head), NY 11545; 516-671-6156.

Central Queens Historical Society, PO Box N, Kew Gardens, NY 11415; 718-544-1737.

Coe Hall Preservation Associates, PO Box 58, Oyster Bay, NY 11771;
    516-922-0479, fax, 922-9226.
Cow Neck Peninsula Historical Society, 336 Port Washington Blvd.,
    Port Washington, NY 11050; 516-365-9074.
Cutchogue-New Suffolk Historical Council, PO Box 714, Cutchogue,
    NY 11935; 516-734-6973 or 734-7211.
Douglaston/Little Neck Historical Society, 28 Shore Road, Douglaston,
    NY 11363.
East Hampton Historical Society, 101 Main St., East Hampton, NY
    11937; 516-324-6850.
East Islip Historical Society, PO Box 585, East Islip, NY 11730.
Eastville Community Historical Society, PO Box 2036, Sag Harbor, NY
    11936.
Farmingdale-Bethpage Historical Society, Box 500, Farmingdale, NY
    11735; 516-249-7856.
Farmingville Historical Society, PO Box 311, Farmingville, NY 11738.
Flatbush Historical Society, 2255 Church Ave., Brooklyn, NY
    11226-3201; 718-856-3700.
Franklin Square Historical Society, PO Box 45, Franklin Square, NY
    11010.
Freeport Historical Society and Museum, 350 S. Main St., Freeport, NY
    11520; 516-623-9632.
Friends for Long Island's Heritage, 1864 Muttontown Rd., Syosset,
    NY 11791; 516-571-7600.
Friends of Historic St. George's Church, PO Box 93, Hempstead, NY
    11551; 516-486-3810.
Friends of Raynham Hall, 20 West Main St., Oyster Bay, NY 11771;
    516-922-6808.
Friends of Rock Hall, PO Box 93 (199 Broadway), Lawrence, NY
    11771; 516-239-1157.
Garden City Historical Society, PO Box 179, Garden City, NY 11530.
Glen Cove Historical Society, c/o Public Library, Glen Cove Ave., Glen
    Cove, NY 11542; 516-676-2130.
Gravesend Historical Society, PO Box 1643, Gravesend, NY 11223;
    718-375-6831.
Greenlawn-Centerport Historical Association, PO Box 354 (31 Broad-
    way), Greenlawn, NY 11740; 516-754-1180.
Greenport—see Stirling Historical Society.
Hempstead Village Historical Society, c/o Hempstead Public Library,
    115, Nichols Ct., Hempstead, NY 11550; 516-481-6990.
Historical Society of . . . [look under name of community].
Huntington Historical Society, 209 Main St., Huntington, NY 11743;
    516-427-7045; fax 427-7056.
Islip Hamlet Historical Society, PO Box 601, Islip, NY 11751.
Ketcham Inn Foundation, Inc., PO Box 626, Center Moriches, NY
    11934.
Lake Ronkonkoma Historical Society, Box 2716, Lake Ronkonkoma,
    NY 11779; 516-467-3152.
Levittown Historical Society, PO Box 57, Levittown, NY 11756;
    516-735-2055/731-5337.

Lindenhurst Historical Society, PO Box 296 (215 S. Wellwood Ave.), Lindenhurst, NY 11757; 516-957-4385.

Lloyd Harbor Historical Society (1711 House, 41 Lloyd Harbor Road), PO Box 582, Lloyd Harbor, NY 11743; 516-424-6110/549-6987.

Locust Valley Historical Society, c/o Public Library, 170 Buckram Rd., Locust Valley, NY 11560; 516-671-1837.

Long Beach Historical Society, PO Box 286, Long Beach, NY 11561; 516-431-3775/432-1192.

Long Island Archives Conference, c/o Peggy McMullen, St. Johns University, Archives, Jamaica, NY 11439; 718-990-6734, fax 718-380-0353.

Long Island Council for the Social Studies (LICSS), PO Box 348, East Setauket, NY 11733-0348.

Long Island Early Fliers Club, PO Box 221, Bethpage, NY 11714; 516-351-1586.

Long Island Republic Airport Historical Society, Terminal Bldg., Republic Airport, Farmingdale, NY 11735; 516-752-7707.

Long Island Studies Council, c/o Long Island Studies Institute, Hofstra University West Campus, 619 Fulton Ave., Hempstead, NY 11550-4575; 516-463-5846/6411 (LISI).

Long Island Studies Institute, Hofstra University West Campus, 619 Fulton Ave., Hempstead, NY 11550-4575; 516-463-6411.

Long Island-Sunrise Trail Chapter, National Historical Railway Society, PO Box 507, Babylon, NY 11702-0507; 516-661-3463.

Long Island Traditions, 619 Brooklyn Ave., Baldwin, NY 11510; 623-5099.

Lynbrook Historical Committee, c/o Lynbrook Public Library, Elder St., Lynbrook, NY 11563; 516-599-8630.

Malverne Historical Society and Preservation Society, PO Box 393, Malverne, NY 11565; 516-599-6639.

Manorville Historical Society, PO Box 4, Manorville, NY 11949-0004.

Massapequas, Historical Society of, PO Box 211 (Old Grace Church, 4755 Merrick Rd.), Massapequa, NY 11758; 516-798-9272.

Mattituck Historical Society, PO Box 766 (Main Road), Mattituck, NY 11952; 516-298-5248/9437.

Merricks, Historical Society of, 2279 Merrick Ave., Merrick, NY 11566; 516-379-1887.

Miller Place Historical Society, Box 651 (1720 William Miller House, North Country Road), Miller Place, NY 11764.

Mineola Historical Society, c/o Memorial Library, Marcellus Road, Mineola, NY 11501; 516-746-2695.

Montauk Historical Society, PO Box 943, Montauk, NY 11954; 516-668-5340 (Montauk Point Lighthouse, 668-2544 and Second House Museum).

Moriches Bay Historical Society, PO Box 31 (Montauk Highway), Center Moriches, NY 11934; 516-878-1776.

Nassau County Division of Museum Services, Department of Parks, Eisenhower Park, East Meadow, NY 11554; 516-572-0254.

Nassau County Historical Society, PO Box 207, Garden City, NY 11530; 516-735-4783.

New York State Archaeological Association, Inc., Long Island Chapter, PO Box 268, Southold, NY 11971; 516-765-5577.

New York State Department of Parks, Recreation, and Historic Preservation, Long Island Region (Belmont Lake State Park), Box 247, Babylon, NY 11702-0247.

North Hempstead Town, Historical Society of, 461 Newton St., Westbury, NY 11590; 516-333-3151.

Northport Historical Society, PO Box 545 (215 Main St.), Northport, NY 11768; 516-757-9859.

Old Field, Village of, Historical Society, PO Box 2724, Setauket, NY 11733.

Oyster Bay Historical Society, PO Box 297 (Earle-Wightman House, 20 Summit St.), Oyster Bay, NY 11791; 516-922-5032.

Oysterponds Historical Society, PO Box 844 (Village Lane), Orient, NY 11957; 516-323-2480.

Patchogue Historical Society, Greater, PO Box 102, Patchogue, NY 11772.

Port Jefferson Historical Society, Box 586 (115 Prospect St.), Port Jefferson, NY 11777; 516-473-2665.

Port Washington—see Cow Neck.

Queens Genealogy Workshop—see Ridgewood Historical Society

Queens Historical Society, 143-35-37th Ave., Flushing, NY 11357; 718-939-0647.

Quogue Historical Society, PO Box 1207 (Old Schoolhouse Museum, Quogue St.), Quogue, NY 11959; 516-643-4111.

Ridgewood, Historical Society of, 1820 Flushing Avenue, Ridgewood, NY 11385-1041; 718-456-1776.

Roslyn Landmark Society, William Valentine House, Paper Mill Rd., Roslyn, NY 11576; 516-621-2961, 621-3040, or 484-1643.

Sag Harbor Historical Society, PO Box 1709 (Long Wharf), Sag Harbor, NY 11936; 516-725-5092.

Sagtikos Manor Historical Society, Box 344, Bay Shore, NY 11706; 516-661-8348.

Sayville Historical Society, PO Box 41 (Edward's House Museum, 39 Edwards St.), Sayville, NY 11782; 516-563-0186.

Sea Cliff Landmarks Association, PO Box 69, Sea Cliff, NY 11579.

Seaford Historical Society, 2234 Jackson Ave., Seaford, NY 11783; 516-826-1150.

Shelter Island Historical Society, PO Box 847 (16 S. Ferry Rd., Route 114), Shelter Island, NY 11964; 516-749-1116/749-0025.

Smithtown Historical Society, PO Box 69 (North Country Rd., Route 25A), Smithtown, NY 11787; 516-265-6768.

Society for the Preservation of Long Island Antiquities (SPLIA), 93 North Country Rd., Setauket, NY 11733; 516-941-9444.

Southampton Historical Society, 17 Meeting House Lane, Southampton, NY 11968; 516-283-2494.

Southold Historical Society, PO Box 1 (54325 Main Road), Southold, NY 11971; 516-765-5500.

Springs Historical Society, PO Box 1860, East Hampton, NY 11937.

Stirling Historical Society, PO Box 590 (Monsell Park), Greenport, NY 11944.

Suffolk County Archaeological Association, PO Drawer 1542, Stony Brook, NY 11790; 516-929-8725.

Suffolk County Division of Historical Services, PO Box 144, West Sayville, NY 11796; 516-854-4970.

Suffolk County Historical Society, 300 W. Main St., Riverhead, NY 11901; 516-727-2881.

Suffolk County Police Historical Society, PO Box 343, Yaphank, NY 11980; 852-6012.

Theodore Roosevelt Association, PO Box 719, Oyster Bay, NY 11771; 516-921-6319.

Three Village Historical Society, PO Box 76, East Setauket, NY 11735; 516-751-3730.

Uniondale Historical Society, 599 Northern Pkwy., Uniondale, NY 11553; 516-485-7456.

Valley Stream Historical Society, PO Box 22 (Pagan-Fletcher Restoration, 143 Hendrickson Ave.), Valley Stream, NY 11582; 516-872-4159.

Wading River Historical Society, PO Box 263 (North Country Road), Wading River, NY 11792; 516-929-4082.

Walt Whitman Birthplace Association, 246 Old Walt Whitman Rd., Huntington Station, NY 11746; 516-427-5240.

Wantagh Preservation Society, PO Box 132, Wantagh, NY 11793; 516-826-8767.

Westburys, Historical Society of, 454 Rockland St., Westbury, NY 11590; 516-333-0176.

Westhampton Beach Historical Society, PO Box 686, Westhampton, NY 11978.

West Hempstead Historical Society and Preservation Society, PO Box 61, West Hempstead, NY 11552; 516-489-6765.

Whaling Museum Society, Inc., PO Box 25, Main Street, Cold Spring Harbor, NY 11724; 516-367-3418.

Yaphank Historical Society, PO Box 111, Yaphank, NY 11980; 516-924-3401.

Long Island Environmental Organizations

Audubon Society, PO Box 735, Huntington, NY 11743, 516-271-8423. Also groups in Bayport, Center Moriches, East Setauket, and Mattituck.

Long Island Greenbelt Trail Conference, 23 Deer Path Road, Central Islip, NY 11722.

Long Island Pine Barrens Society, 97 Lakeside Trail, Ridge, NY 11961.

Nature Conservancy, Long Island Chapter, Lawrence Hill Road, Cold Spring Harbor, NY 11724; 516-367-3225.

Save the Peconic Bays, Inc., Box 449, Mattituck, NY 11952; 516-298-4620.

Sierra Club, Long Island Chapter, Box 210, Syosset, NY 11791.

Theodore Roosevelt Sanctuary, Cove Road, Oyster Bay, NY; 922-3200.

Museums and Historic Houses

This list is not exhaustive; many of the historical societies (see list above) also have museums. Some of the museums are seasonal—telephone for hours and fees (area code is 516 unless otherwise noted). A more complete list of museums in Nassau County appears in the Institute's *Roots and Heritage of Hempstead Town*, 220-24. Descriptions of museums are in Bernie Bookbinder, *Long Island: People and Places, Past and Present* (1983), 246-54; Raymond Spinzia, Judith Spinzia, and Kathryn Spinzia, *Long Island: A Guide to New York's Suffolk and Nassau Counties* (1988; rev. ed. 1991); SCOPE, *Where to Go and What to Do on Long Island* (1993); and the Long Island Museum Association (LIMA) brochure, *Long Island Museums and Historical Societies Guide* (1994).

African American Museum, 110 N. Franklin St., Hempstead, 11550; 572-0730.

American Merchant Marine Museum, U.S. Merchant Marine Academy, Steamboat Rd., Kings Point, 11024; 773-5515, fax 482-5340.

Babylon Museum, Town of, 151 Phelps Lane, North Babylon, 11703; 893-2179, fax 893-2123.

Bayville Museum, 34 School Street, Bayville, 11709; 628-1720, fax 628-3740.

Bellport-Brookhaven Historical Society Museum complex, 31 Bellport Lane, Bellport, 11713; 286-0888.

Big Duck, Route 24, Hampton Bays, 11796; 852-8292.

BNL Science Museum, Brookhaven National Laboratory, Upton, 11973-5000; 282-4049, fax 282-7098.

Bowne House, 37-91 Bowne Street, Flushing, 11354; 718-359-0528.

Bridgehampton Museum, Main Street, Bridgehampton, 11932; 537-1008.

Brooklyn Historical Society, 128 Pierrepont St., Brooklyn Hgts., 11201; 718-624-0890.

Brooklyn Museum, Eastern Parkway at Washington Ave., Brooklyn; 718-638-5000.

Centerport, Barn Museum and Suydam House, 1 Fort Salonga Rd., Centerport, 11740; Greenlawn-Centerport Historical Association, 754-1180.

Coe Hall (c. 1920) at Planting Fields Arboretum/State Historic Park, Planting Fields Road (PO Box 58), Oyster Bay, 11771; 922-9210, fax 922-9226.

Coindre Hall, see Gold Coast Museum.

Cold Spring Harbor Whaling Museum, Main St. (Rt. 25A) at Turkey
    Lane (PO Box 25), Cold Spring Harbor 11724; 367-3418.
Cradle of Aviation Museum, Mitchel Field, Garden City, 11530;
    572-0411. Closed 1994 for major renovations.
Custom House (c. 1790), Main & Garden Streets, Sag Harbor 11963;
    941-9444 (SPLIA).
Cutchogue Green Complex (includes Old House, c. 1649, Wickham
    House, c. 1740, 1840 schoolhouse), Main Road, Cutchogue, 19935;
    734-7122.
Deepwells, North Country (Route 25A) and Moriches Roads, St.
    James 11780; information 854-4970.
DNA Learning Center, 334 Main St. (Route 25A), Cold Spring Harbor,
    11724-2219; 367-7240. Features *Long Island Discovery*, a 28 min.
    multi-media presentation on Long Island.
Earle-Wightman House, 20 Summit St. (Oyster Bay Historical Society,
    PO Box 297), Oyster Bay 11771; 922-5032.
East Hampton Historical Society (Osborn-Jackson House, Clinton
    Academy, Mulford Farm, Town Marine Museum) 101 Main
    Street, East Hampton, 11937; 324-6850.
Edwards House, 39 Edwards St. (Sayville Historical Society), Sayville,
    11782.
Falaise at Sands Point Preserve, Middleneck Rd., Port Washington,
    11050; 883-1610, fax 883-0635. Guggenheim's 1923 Gold Coast
    estate; also Hempstead House and Castlegould.
Fine Arts Museum of Long Island, 295 Fulton Ave., Hempstead,
    11550; 481-5700.
Freeport Historical Society, 350 South Main St., Freeport 11520;
    623-9632.
Garvies Point Museum and Preserve, Barry Drive, Glen Cove, 11542;
    571-8010. Long Island geology, archaeology, and Indian culture.
Gold Coast, Museum of Long Island's, Coindre Hall, 101 Browns
    Road, Huntington, 11743; 424-8230 or 854-4970.
Goudreau Museum of Mathematics in Art and Science—The Math
    Museum, Herricks Road at junction of Shelter Rock and
    Searingtown Rd, New Hyde Park, 11040; 747-0777.
Gregory Museum, Long Island Earth Science Center, Heitz Place and
    Bay Ave, Hicksville, 11801; 822-7505.
Guild Hall (fine arts museum), 158 Main Street, East Hampton, 11937;
    324-0806, fax 324-2722.
Hallockville Museum Farm, 163 Sound Avenue, Riverhead, 11901;
    298-5292.
Heckscher Museum, 2 Prime Avenue (Heckscher Park), Huntington,
    11743; 351-3250, fax 423-2145.
Hofstra Museum, 112 Hofstra University, Fulton Ave, Hempstead
    11550-1090; 463-5672, fax 463-4832. Exhibits in Emily Lowe,
    Filderman, and Lowenstein galleries; outdoor sculpture.
Home Sweet Home Museum (c. 1660), 14 James Lane, East Hampton,
    11937; 342-0713.
Huntington Historical Society, 209 Main St. (Library), Huntington,
    11743; 427-7045, fax 427-7056. Conklin Farmhouse (c. 1750) on

New York Ave. (Rt. 110) at High St. and Kissam House (c. 1795), 434 Park Ave.

Islip Art Museum, 50 Irish Lane, East Islip, 11730; 224-5402, fax 224-5440.

Islip Grange, 10 Broadway, Sayville, 11782; open for special events, 224-5411. Restored houses and buildings.

Joseph Lloyd Manor House (c. 1766), Lloyd Harbor Rd., Lloyd Neck 11743; 941-9444.

King Manor Museum, King Park, 150th St. and Jamaica Avenue (mailing address: 90-04-161st St., Suite 704), Jamaica, 11432; 718-291-0282.

Kingsland House (1785), 143-35 37th Ave., Flushing; home of Queens Historical Society with period rooms and changing exhibits; 718-939-0647.

Lauder Museum, PO Box 764 (170 Broadway), Amityville, 11701; 598-1486.

Long Island Children's Museum, 550 Stewart Ave., Garden City, 11530; 222-0217, fax 222-0225.

Long Island Maritime Museum, 86 West Ave. (south of Montauk Highway, adjacent to County Golf Course, PO Box 184), West Sayville, 11796; 854-4974, fax 854-4979.

Long Island Republic Airport Historical Society, exhibits in Republic Airport lobby, Route 110, Farmingdale, 11735; 669-7395.

Manor of St. George, Neighborhood Rd., Mastic; 475-0327.

Meadow Croft, Sayville. Information: 854-4970.

Miller House (1720), North Country Road (PO Box 651), Miller Place, 11764.

Museum of Long Island Natural Sciences, ESS Building, SUNY Stony Brook, Stony Brook, 11794; 632-8230.

Museums at Stony Brook, 1208 Route 25A, Stony Brook, 11790; 751-0066, fax 751-0353. Art, carriage, and history museums, schoolhouse and blacksmith shop; changing exhibits, always some William Sidney Mount paintings on exhibit.

Nassau County Museum of Art, 1 Museum Drive (off Northern Blvd) (PO Box D), Roslyn Harbor, 11576; 484-9338, fax 484-0710.

Nassau County Police Museum, Police Headquarters, 1490 Franklin Ave., Mineola, 11501; 573-7000.

Northport Historical Museum, 215 Main St., Northport, 11768; 757-9859.

Old Bethpage Village Restoration, Round Swamp Road, Old Bethpage 11804; 572-8400, fax 572-8413.

Old Westbury House (1906) and Gardens, 71 Old Westbury Rd., Old Westbury, 11568; 333-0048.

Oysterponds Historical Society, museum complex, Village Lane, Orient, 11957; 323-2480.

Parrish Art Museum, 25 Job's Lane, Southampton, 11968; 283-2118, fax 283-7006.

Phillips House, Museum of the Village of Rockville Centre, 28 Hempstead Ave., Rockville Centre, 11571; 766-0300.

Pollock-Krasner House and Study Center, 830 Fireplace Road, East Hampton, 11937; 324-4929.

Queens County Farm Museum, 73-50 Little Neck Parkway, Floral Park, 11004; 718-347-3276.

Queens Museum, Flushing Meadow Corona Park, Flushing, 11368; 718-592-5555.

Raynham Hall Museum (c. 1733), 20 W. Main St., Oyster Bay 11771; 922-6808, fax 922-6808.

Rock Hall (1767), 199 Broadway (PO Box 93), Lawrence 11559; 239-1157.

Sagamore Hill National Historic Site, TR's home and Old Orchard Museum, Sagamore Hill Rd., Oyster Bay, 11771; 922-4447.

Sag Harbor Whaling Museum, Main & Garden St., Sag Harbor, 11963; 725-0770.

Sagtikos Manor, Route 27A, West Bay Shore; 661-8348.

Science Museum of Long Island, 1526 Plandome Rd., Manhasset, 11030; 627-9400.

Sea Cliff Village Museum, 95 Tenth Street (PO Box 72) Sea Cliff, 11579; 671-0090.

Shinnecock National Museum Cultural Center Complex, Shinnecock Reservation, PO Box 59, Southampton, 11969; 287-4923/4688, fax 287-4978. Under development.

Smithtown Historical Society, Caleb Smith House and Epenetus Smith Tavern, Route 25A (PO Box 69), Smithtown, 11787; 265-6768.

Society for the Preservation of Long Island Antiquities (SPLIA) Gallery, Main St. at Shore Rd., Cold Spring Harbor 11724; 367-6295/941-9444. SPLIA also maintains Custom House, Joseph Lloyd Manor House, Sherwood-Jayne and Thompson Houses.

Southampton Historical Society Museum complex, 17 Meeting House Lane, Southampton, 11968; 283-2494.

Southold Historical Museums, 54325 Main St., Southold, 11971; 765-5500.

Southold Indian Museum, Bayview Road (PO Box 268), Southold, 11971; 765-5577.

Suffolk County Historical Society, 300 W. Main St., Riverhead 11901; 727-2881. Permanent and changing exhibits.

Suffolk County Police Museum, Police Headquarters, Yaphank Ave., Yaphank; 345-6011/6012.

Tackapausha Museum and Preserve, Washington Ave., Seaford 11783; 571-7443.

Telephone Museum, 445 Commack Rd., Commack, 11725; 543-1371.

Thompson House, 91 N. Country Rd., Setauket; 941-9444 (SPLIA).

Vanderbilt Museum of Suffolk County, 180 Little Neck Rd. (PO Box 0605), Centerport, 11721; 854-5555, fax 854-5527.

Walt Whitman Birthplace Museum, 246 Old Walt Whitman Rd., Huntington Station, 11746; 427-5240, fax 427-5247.

William Floyd Estate, 245 Park Drive, Mastic Beach 11951; 399-2030. National Historic Park Site, home of signer of Declaration of Independence.

Chronology of Long Island History

1524	Giovanni Verrazano sails along the South Shore of Long Island
1609	Some of Henry Hudson's crew from *de Halve Maen* land on Coney Island
1614	Adrian Block sails through Hellsgate to Long Island Sound; maps and names "Lange Eilandt"
1621	Dutch West India Company receives charter
1624	First Dutch settlements on Manhattan and Nutte (Governor's) Island
1636	Dutch settle in Gowanus and Nieuw Amersfoort (Flatlands)
1638	Ferry service established between Breuckelen and New Amsterdam across East River
1639	Lion and Mary Willemsan Gardiner move from Connecticut to the Isle of Wight (Gardiners Island), land received from Lord Sterling and Wyandanch
1640	English from New England settle Southold and Southampton
1643	Lady Deborah Moody and followers establish Gravesend, the first English settlement in western Long Island
1643–44	Indian uprising (Kieft's war) in western Long Island
1643–44	English families from Connecticut purchase land from the Indians, receive patent from Dutch authorities, and settle Hempstead
1645	Vlissingen (Flushing) founded
1645	Breucklen established as a town
1648	East Hampton settled
1650	Treaty of Hartford divides Long Island between Dutch and English (about four miles west of the present-day Nassau-Suffolk boundary)
1656	Rustdorp (Jamaica) receives charter
1656	Elizabeth Garlick of East Hampton accused of witchcraft; is found not guilty after trial in Connecticut
1657	Flushing Remonstrance welcomes Quakers, despite widespread persecution of members of the Society of Friends
1662	John Bowne arrested for permitting Quakers to worship in his Flushing home, but acquitted after trial in the Netherlands; a victory for religious toleration

1664	Dutch surrender New Netherland to English; colony renamed New York
1665	Duke's Laws Convention in Hempstead establishes laws for governance of the colony
1665	Gov. Richard Nicolls set up the New Market race course on the Hempstead Plains
1673–74	Dutch recapture New Netherland, but cede back to the English fifteen months later in peace settlement
1683	Suffolk, Queens, and Kings counties established
1692	New York Assembly renames Long Island the "Island of Nassau"
1695	Thomas Powell makes Bethpage Purchase
1703	King's Highway (present-day Jamaica Ave.) authorized by province
1766	Sons of Liberty in Oyster Bay protest British stamp tax
1774	First Continental Congress in Philadelphia passes embargo on British goods; eastern Long Island supports, but many in western Long Island oppose
1775	Whigs in northern part of the Town of Hempstead declare independence from rest of town where Loyalists in the majority; would officially divide in 1784 into North and South Hempstead confirming schism
1776	First blood shed on Long Island in the Battle of Hempstead Swamp (a skirmish in what is now Tanglewood Preserve), June 22-23
1776	William Floyd of Mastic, Francis Lewis, a retired merchant living in Whitestone, and Philip Livingston, whose country home was in Brooklyn Heights, are three of four signers of the Declaration of Independence for New York
1776	Battle of Long Island, August 27-29 in Brooklyn Heights; British victorious; Washington and troops successfully retreat to Manhattan; many patriots flee to Connecticut
1776–83	Revolutionary War: Long Island occupied by British and Hessian troops; patriots conduct whaleboat raids from Connecticut and spy network on Long Island; British prison ships anchor in Wallabout Bay (Brooklyn)
1782–83	Thousands of Long Island's Loyalist refugees leave for Canada
1783	Final Long Island evacuation; December 4; last contingent of British troops leave United States
1784	New York State legislature fines Long Island for not taking more active role in the Revolutionary War

1785	Clinton Academy opens in East Hampton
1787	Erasmus Hall (Flatbush) and Clinton Academy receive state charter, first incorporated secondary schools in New York State
1788	New York ratifies United States Constitution; compromise position of Long Island delegate Samuel Jones helps sway votes of anti-Federalists
1789	New federal government designates Sag Harbor port of entry
1790	President George Washington tours Long Island
1791	*Long Island Herald*, first Long Island newspaper, begins in Sag Harbor
1795–96	Montauk lighthouse constructed at eastern end of Long Island
1799	New York State law decrees children of slaves born after July 4, 1799 to be freed; males at age 25 and females at 28
1801	Brooklyn Navy Yard established
1806	First turnpike built on Long Island, links Jamaica and Rockaway
1812–13	School districts established throughout state; each expected to provide tax-supported common (elementary) schools
1812–14	War of 1812: British squadron is anchored in Gardiners Bay and raids Sag Harbor
1814	Jamaica is the first village to be incorporated on Long Island
1814	Steam ferry service begins between Brooklyn and New York
1816	Village of Brooklyn is incorporated; town became a city in 1834
1824	Lighthouse built at western tip of Fire Island
1827	Hicksite schism in the Society of Friends named for Elias Hicks, Quaker from Jericho
1827	All slavery ends in New York State
1830–68	William Sidney Mount, Stony Brook artist, paints portraits and Long Island genre scenes
1834	Long Island Railroad is chartered; provides service to Hicksville by 1836; to Greenport by 1844 (for route to Boston via ferry across Sound)
1836–37	Passenger ships *Bristol* and *Mexico* wrecked off Long Beach and more than 150 lives lost—monument in Rockville Centre Cemetery; many other shipwrecks off Long Island coast over the years
1842	First Queens County Agricultural Fair held at Hempstead

1842	William Cullen Bryant, poet and editor of the *New York Post*, purchases land in Roslyn Harbor for his country home, Cedarmere
1847	Whaling at peak; Sag Harbor and Cold Spring Harbor are important ports
1850	Modern Times, a utopian, anarchist, free love community established by Josiah Warren at present-day Brentwood
1855	Walt Whitman publishes the first edition of *Leaves of Grass*
1859	St. Francis Academy founded in Brooklyn; becomes a college in 1884
1861–62	Benjamin Willis recruits Company H (the "Willis Company"), part of the 119th Regiment which fights in many Civil War battles
1861–65	Camp Winfield Scott, on the Hempstead Plains, is a training ground for Union soldiers
1862	Ironclad warship *Monitor* launched at Greenpoint, Brooklyn
1863	Civil War draft riot in Jamaica
1863	Long Island Historical Society founded; renamed Brooklyn Historical Society in 1985
1864	Women's Relief Association of Long Island sponsors the Brooklyn and Long Island Sanitary Fair at the Brooklyn Academy of Music; raises $400,000 for Union medical services
1869	Alexander T. Stewart purchases over 7,000 acres of Hempstead Plains and establishes Garden City; in 1885, widow Cornelia Clinch Stewart builds cathedral as memorial to her husband
1870	St. John's College established in Brooklyn; opens campus in Jamaica in 1955
1870	Long Island City incorporated
1870–72	Steinway Piano Factory and village established in Astoria
1874	Queens County court house relocates from Mineola to Long Island City
1874	Prospect Park completed in Brooklyn; designed by Frederick Law Olmstead and Calvert Vaux
1883	Brooklyn Bridge opens (construction had begun in 1870); John Roebling and son Washington Roebling, engineers
1885	Brooklyn's first elevated railway completed
1890	Biological Laboratory established in Cold Spring Harbor
1891–1902	William Merritt Chase conducts Shinnecock Summer School of Art in Southampton; Chase painted many Long Island scenes

1892	Shinnecock Hills Gold Club opens, one of first in U.S.
1897	Brooklyn Public Library established
1897	Brooklyn Museum opens
1898	Steeplechase Park, a large amusement park, opens at Coney Island
1898	Camp Black near Mineola and Camp Wikoff at Montauk serve as training grounds in the Spanish-American War; Rough Riders, Theodore Roosevelt's volunteer cavalry unit, returns to Camp Wikoff
1898	Greater New York City established with five boroughs including Brooklyn and the three western towns of Queens (Flushing, Jamaica, and Newtown)
1899	Nassau County established by the three eastern towns of Queens (Hempstead, North Hempstead, and Oyster Bay)
1901–09	Theodore Roosevelt is President of the United States and Sagamore Hill, his home in Oyster Bay, is the summer White House
1901	Guglielmo Marconi, inventor of wireless telegraphy, sends first wireless radio message from Babylon
1903	Williamsburg Bridge opens linking Brooklyn and Manhattan; Manhattan Bridge opens in 1909
1904	Carnegie Institution establishes Station for Experimental Evolution in Cold Spring Harbor
1906	First Vanderbilt Cup automobile race held on Long Island
1908	The Interborough Rapid Transit (IRT) subway connects Manhattan to Brooklyn via Joralemon Street tunnel
1908	William K. Vanderbilt, Jr. constructs the Long Island Motor Parkway (first limited-access concrete road) for Vanderbilt Cup Races
1909	Queensborough Bridge opens, linking Queens and Manhattan
1909	Glenn Curtiss makes pioneering flights on the Hempstead Plains; International Aviation Meet at Belmont Park in 1910
1910	Doubleday publishers move to Garden City
1910	Francis Hodgson Burnett writes *The Secret Garden* in Plandome
1910	Forest Hills Gardens in Queens begins to be developed by the Russell Sage Foundation as a model planned community

1910	Electric train service and tunnels under East River give direct access from Long Island to Manhattan
1911	Brooklyn Botanic Garden opens
1911	Moisant School opens on Hempstead Plains and trains Harriet Quimby, first licensed woman pilot; Cal Rogers in *Vin Fiz* made first coast-to-coast flight (leaving from Sheepshead Bay); first air mail flight (Franklin Square to Mineola) by Earl Ovington
1912	New York Ashcan group of painters attracted to Bellport
1912	New York State School of Agriculture founded at Farmingdale; now four-year SUNY College of Technology
1915	Queensboro subway opens
1917–18	World War I: aviators train at Hazelhurst, Mitchel, and Roosevelt Fields; soldiers at Camp Mills (Garden City) and Camp Upton (Yaphank)
1922	First trans-Atlantic radio telephone transmittal station built by RCA at Rocky Point
1922–24	Novelist F. Scott Fitzgerald writes *The Great Gatsby* while living in Great Neck, and immortalizes the jazz age of the Roaring Twenties and Long Island's Gold Coast
1923	Ku Klux Klan rally in East Islip attracts 25,000
1924	Sunnyside Gardens, a planned apartment complex, opens in Queens
1924	Long Island State Park Commission organized under Robert Moses
1927	Charles Lindbergh departs from Roosevelt Field on first successful non-stop solo flight across Atlantic; lands in Paris
1927	Southern State parkway opens as limited-access road to reach the state parks; first of several parkways built by Robert Moses
1929	Jones Beach State Park opens
1929	Adelphi College moves to Garden City (founded in Brooklyn in 1869, as an academy, it had become a women's college in 1896); became coeducational after World War II
1929	Grumman Aircraft founded in a rented Baldwin garage
1930	Michael Cullen opens King Kullen in Jamaica, first United States supermarket
1930	Brooklyn College founded
1930–31	Big Duck built in Flanders; prototype of "Duck" architecture

1933	Grand Central and Northern State Parkways open
1933–39	WPA Program of New Deal combats unemployment by funding public projects including courthouses, post offices, roads, parks, and murals
1935	Hofstra opens as two-year extension branch of New York University; by 1940, it becomes an independent four-year college
1936	Triborough Bridge opens (construction began in 1929)
1937	Queens College founded
1937–39	Camp Siegfried, German-American Bund (Nazi sympathizers), operates in Yaphank
1938	Hurricane causes severe damage on eastern Long Island; 70 killed
1939	Pan American inaugurates overseas air flights from Manhasset Bay
1939	LaGuardia Airport opens as a land and seaplane terminal
1939	Whitestone Bridge opens
1939–40	New York World's Fair held in Flushing Meadow Park, Queens
1940	Queens Midtown Tunnel opens
1940	*Newsday* begins publication under Alicia Patterson and Harry Guggenheim
1940–45	World War II: Long Island prominent in defense industry with Grumman, Republic, Sperry, Liberty, Brewster, Columbia, Hazeltine, and Fairchild companies
1942	German saboteurs land from submarine at Amagansett
1945	Miracle Mile shopping center opens on Northern Blvd. in Manhasset
1947	Levitt's assembly-line housing development begins the postwar suburban boom on Long Island
1947	Brookhaven National Laboratory established at former Camp Upton in Yaphank
1947	Webb Institute of Naval Architecture moves to Pratt estate in Glen Cove
1951	Roosevelt Field closes as airfield; sold for shopping center
1957	Ebbets Field sold for housing; Dodgers baseball team leaves Brooklyn
1961	Throgs Neck Bridge opens, connecting Bronx and Long Island
1962	SUNY, Stony Brook established; had begun in 1957 as science center at Planting Fields, Oyster Bay

1962	Cold Spring Harbor Laboratory formed by merger of Biological Laboratory (1890) and Carnegie Station (1904); an internationally famous center for genetic research and molecular biology education
1964	World's Fair opens in Flushing Meadow Park, Queens
1964	Verrazano-Narrows Bridge connects Brooklyn and Staten Island
1964	Fire Island National Seashore established
1969	Lunar Modular, built by Grumman on Long Island, lands on moon
1971	Federal government designates Nassau-Suffolk counties a Standard Metropolitan Statistical Area (SMSA); first SMSA without a central city
1971	Gateway National Recreation Area created in Jamaica Bay, Brooklyn
1973	LILCO begins construction of Shoreham atomic energy plant; shut down in 1994 without having operated
1980–83	New York Islanders, based at the Nassau Coliseum, win Stanley Cup Championships in hockey
1981	Alfonse D'Amato of Island Park is elected United States Senator
1983	Barbara McClintock receives Nobel Prize for work in genetics at Cold Spring Harbor Laboratory
1984	Geraldine Ferraro (Forest Hills, Queens) first woman vice presidential candidate for major party
1987	Islip's garbage barge dramatizes problem of disposal of Long Island waste
1988	Republic Aviation, acquired by Fairchild in 1965, is closed and Farmingdale plant sold for shopping center
1994	Grumman Aerospace acquired by Northrop
1994	Nassau County voters approve new legislature

Population Statistics

Present-day Nassau County was part of Queens until 1899.
After the three western towns joined New York City in 1898, the
three eastern towns became a separate county. There were some

Table 1
Population by County, 1790–1990

Year	Kings	Bklyn*	Queens	Nassau*	Suffolk	Total
1790	4,495	1,653	16,014	10,621	16,440	36,949
1800	5,740	2,378	16,961	11,102	19,735	42,436
1810	8,303	5,200	19,336	12,509	21,113	48,752
1820	11,187	7,302	21,519	n.a.	23,930	56,636
1830	20,535	15,394	22,460	14,470	26,780	69,775
1840	47,613	36,236	30,324	17,365	32,469	110,406
1850	138,882	96,838	36,833	20,002	36,922	212,637
1860	279,122	266,661	57,391	26,963	43,275	379,788
1870	419,921	396,099	73,803	31,134	46,924	540,648
1880	599,495	566,663	90,574	37,647	53,888	743,957
1890	838,547	806,343	128,059	45,760	62,491	1,029,097
1900	1,166,582		152,999	55,448	77,582	1,452,611
1910	1,634,351		284,041	83,930	96,138	2,098,460
1920	2,018,356		469,042	126,120	110,246	2,723,764
1930	2,560,401		1,019,129	303,053	161,055	4,043,638
1940	2,698,285		1,297,634	406,748	197,355	4,600,022
1950	2,738,175		1,550,849	672,765	276,129	5,237,918
1960	2,637,319		1,809,578	1,300,171	666,784	6,413,852
1970	2,602,012		1,987,174	1,428,838	1,127,030	7,145,054
1980	2,230,936		1,891,325	1,321,582	1,284,231	6,728,074
1990	2,300,664		1,951,598	1,287,348	1,321,864	6,861,474

*Brooklyn's population is included in the totals for Kings County though it is also listed
separately, 1790–1890; similarly, Nassau population is included in Queens County's,
1790–1890. Hence, the total population for geographical Long Island in the last column
is the sum of Kings, Queens, and Suffolk Counties for 1790–1990 and Kings, Queens,
Nassau, and Suffolk, 1890–1990.

changes in the western boundary line of the Town of Hempstead at this time, most notably with the Rockaway peninsula becoming part of New York City.

Brooklyn was one of the original six towns when Kings County was created in 1683. Table 1 shows its urban growth after 1820; it became a city in 1834 and expanded its boundaries over the years. Brooklyn became coterminous with the county (or borough) when it consolidated with greater New York in 1898.

In the colonial period, Queens and Suffolk had a larger population (as well as area) than Kings County. Table 2 shows the population of the Long Island counties, 1698–1786, with totals for the island and province of New York.

Table 2
Population of Queens, Suffolk, and Kings Counties, Long Island, and New York, 1698–1786

Year	Queens	Suffolk	Kings	Long Island	New York
1698	3,565	2,679	2,017	8,261	18,067
1703	4,392	3,346	1,912	9,650	20,665
1723	7,191	6,241	2,218	15,650	40,564
1731	7,995	7,675	2,150	17,820	50,286
1737	9,059	7,923	2,348	19,330	60,437
1746	9,640	9,254	2,331	21,225	61,589
1749	7,940	9,384	2,283	19,607	73,448
1756	10,786	10,290	2,707	22,783	96,590
1771	10,980	13,128	3,623	27,731	168,017
1786	13,084	13,793	3,986	30,863	238,897

Sources: 1698–1890, James E. Bunce and Richard P. Harmond, eds. *Long Island as America: A Documentary History to 1896* (Port Washington, NY: Kennikat, 1977), 187; Brooklyn, 1900–1980, Margaret Latimer, ed. *Brooklyn Almanac* (Brooklyn: Brooklyn Rediscovery, 1984), 24; Nassau, 1790–1980 and Suffolk, 1900–1980, *Historical Population of Long Island Communities, 1790–1980* (Hauppauge, NY: Long Island Regional Planning Board, 1982), 15–16; Queens, 1900–1940, *A Research Guide to the History of the Borough of Queens*, ed. Jon A. Peterson (Queens, History Department, Queens College, 1987), 13; and 1940–1990 statistics, *U.S. Census of Population and Housing: New York* (Washington, DC: Bureau of the Census, 1990), 1: 3. Consult these sources for population of towns or specific communities; detailed information is in decennial census reports.

Editors and Contributors

LYNDA DAY currently teaches Africana Studies at Brooklyn College of the City University of New York. She was curator of Nassau County's African American Museum in Hempstead from 1983 to 1988.

CHARLES F. HOWLETT has taught social studies in the Amityville public schools since 1977 and was district director of social studies from 1986-1992. He has a Ph.D. in American History from SUNY at Albany and is an adjunct professor at Adelphi University. He has written numerous articles and a number of books including *Brookwood Labor College and the Struggle for Peace and Social Justice in America, 1917-1937* (1993) and *The American Peace Movement: References and Resources* (1991). He is co-author of two local histories, *A Walk Through History: A Community Named Amityville* (1993) and *Amityville's 1894 School House* (1994).

JOANN B. KRIEG teaches English and American Studies at Hofstra University where she is Associate Professor of English. She is the author of *Long Island and Literature* (1989) and *Epidemics in the Modern World* (1992). Other Institute books she has edited are *Evoking a Sense of Place* (1988), *Robert Moses: Single-Minded Genius* (1989), and *Long Island Architecture* (1991). Dr. Krieg is also editor of *Walt Whitman, Here and Now* (1985).

LAURA MACDERMEID was the Education Curator at the Huntington Historical Society when she spoke at the Institute conference on the Society's school program. For more than five years she was College for Children Coordinator at LaGuardia Community College's Division of Continuing Education and is currently Community School Coordinator at P.S. 38 in Brooklyn.

DAVID BUNN MARTINE who did the illustrations for the article on Indians is a Native American artist whose ancestry is Shinnecock and Apache. He is currently with the Smithsonian's National Museum of the American Indian in New York City.

NATALIE A. NAYLOR teaches American social history in Hofstra University's New College and is director of the Long Island Studies Institute. Other Institute publications which she has edited are *Exploring African-American History* (1991), *Roots and Heritage of Hempstead Town* (1994), and *Theodore Roosevelt: Many-Sided American* (co-editor, 1992). She has published a number of articles on educational history and Long Island history.

MELISSA PATTON was Associate Director for Education at The Parrish Art Museum from 1984 to 1990. She developed interpretive materials, including slide-cassette kits on Long Island artists and architecture, and directed the collaborative project with the Bridgehampton School described in *Long Island's History and Cultural Heritage*.

DOROTHY B. RUETTGERS taught elementary school in the Farmingdale School District. She has degrees in history, English, and education and is currently Adjunct Assistant Professor at Hofstra University where she teaches writing and children's literature. She has spoken at several Long Island Studies Institute conferences, most recently on "Long Island's Heritage for Students of All Ages" (1994).

ROSEMARY SLOGGATT received her bachelor's degree from Parson's School of Design and her master's from Bank Street College of Education. She has been a museum educator at the Museum of Modern Art, the Cold Spring Harbor Whaling Museum, and the Huntington Historical Society.

JOHN A. STRONG is professor of American Studies and Director of Social Science Division at the Southampton Campus of Long Island University. He has written extensively on Long Island Indians and is preparing a book for the Institute on the topic.

The Long Island Studies Institute

The Long Island Studies Institute is a cooperative endeavor of Hofstra University and Nassau County. This major center for the study of local and regional history was established in 1985 to foster the study of Long Island history and heritage. Two major research collections on the study of Nassau County, Long Island and New York State are located in the Special Collections Department on the University's West Campus, 619 Fulton Avenue, Hempstead. These collections—the Nassau County Museum collection and Hofstra University's James N. MacLean American Legion Memorial collection—are available to historians, librarians, teachers, and the general public, as well as to Hofstra students and faculty. Together, they offer a rich repository of books, photographs, newspapers, maps, census records, genealogies, government documents, manuscripts, and audiovisual materials.

In addition to its research collections, the Institute sponsors publications, meetings, and conferences pertaining to Long Island and its heritage. Through its programs, the Institute complements various Long Island Studies courses offered by the University through the History Department, New College, and University College for Continuing Education.

The Long Island Studies Institute is open Monday-Friday (except major holidays) 9–5 (Fridays to 4 in the summer). For further information, contact the Institute, 516-463-6409/6411. The Institute also houses the historical research offices of the Nassau County Historian and Division of Museum Services (516-463-6417.)

Long Island Studies Institute Publications

Heart of the Lakes Publishing:

The Aerospace Heritage of Long Island, by Joshua Stoff (1989).
The Blessed Isle: Hal B. Fullerton and His Image of Long Island, 1897-1927, by Charles L. Sachs (1991).
Evoking a Sense of Place, ed. Joann P. Krieg (1988).